B·A·S·E·B·A·L·L
STARS
1985

DAN SCHLOSSBERG

CONTEMPORARY
BOOKS, INC.
CHICAGO

Library of Congress Cataloging in Publication Data

Schlossberg, Dan, 1948—
    Baseball stars, 1985.

    1. Baseball players—United States—Biography.
I. Title.
GV865.A1S33   1985   796.357′092′2 [B]   85-413
ISBN 0-8092-5268-6

To Suzanne, Cody, and Samantha,
who patiently endured the isolation and separation
that made this book possible

Photo credits:

Photos on pages 14 and 15 by R. Mironovich; on pages 16, 17, 18,
73, 74, 85, 86 and 87 by Jerry Wachter; on page 20 by Dennis
Desprois; on pages 23 and 80 by Arne Glassbourg; on page 38 by
Kevin W. Reece; on pages 89, 90, 100, 101, and 102 by Stephen
Green; on page 92 by Paul H. Roedig; on page 99 courtesy of
Action Photographics, Inc.; and on page 208 courtesy of Todd
Studios, Inc.

Published by Contemporary Books, Inc.
180 North Michigan Avenue, Chicago, Illinois 60601
Library of Congress Catalog Card Number: 85-413
Manufactured in the United States of America
International Standard Book Number: 0-8092-5268-6

Published simultaneously in Canada by Beaverbooks, Ltd.
195 Allstate Parkway, Valleywood Business Park
Markham, Ontario L3R 4T8 Canada

CONTENTS

FOREWORD iv

PREFACE v

JOAQUIN ANDUJAR 1

TONY ARMAS 4

HAROLD BAINES 7

BUDDY BELL 10

BERT BLYLEVEN 13

MIKE BODDICKER 16

BOB BRENLY 19

GARY CARTER 22

JOSE CRUZ 25

ALVIN DAVIS 28

STEVE GARVEY 31

KIRK GIBSON 34

DWIGHT GOODEN 37

GOOSE GOSSAGE 40

TONY GWYNN 43

KEITH HERNANDEZ 46

WILLIE HERNANDEZ 49

KENT HRBEK 52

DAVE KINGMAN 55

MARK LANGSTON 58

DON MATTINGLY 61

LARRY McWILLIAMS 64

JACK MORRIS 67

DALE MURPHY 70

EDDIE MURRAY 73

DAN QUISENBERRY 76

TIM RAINES 79

JIM RICE 82

CAL RIPKEN 85

RYNE SANDBERG 88

MIKE SCHMIDT 91

MARIO SOTO 94

DAVE STEIB 97

RICK SUTCLIFFE 100

BRUCE SUTTER 103

ALAN TRAMMELL 106

FERNANDO VALENZUELA 109

DAVE WINFIELD 112

MIKE WITT 115

ROBIN YOUNT 118

1984 LEAGUE STANDINGS 121

ACKNOWLEDGMENTS 122

FOREWORD

For most people, baseball is a game that intrigues its public for six months—from spring training through the World Series. Not for my friend Dan Schlossberg, though. To Dan, baseball happens 365 days out of the year—and for a lifetime.

He is dedicated to baseball. He has followed it assiduously almost all his life and he writes about it constantly. I believe that he even dodges fastballs in his sleep. Such dedication in Dan has developed him into one of the outstanding authorities on the game he loves. And for Dan, baseball is the only game. All the others are imposters.

His credentials are outstanding. He has been a newspaper writer, editor, radio and TV writer, and author of several outstanding books. I thought his *The Baseball Catalog* was one of the best and most comprehensive of all baseball books. And his *The Baseball Book of Why* explains a lot of origins to many of us who had wondered about those diamond beginnings but had never had the ingenuity or know-how of a Dan Schlossberg. He found out about them for all of us.

Now, in his sixth book, Dan is bringing to us in his own, original, distinctive way, miniprofiles of some of the top current stars in baseball. We could ask for no better guide to take us on the trip to explore the background of the diamond greats.

Over my 38 years of big-league broadcasting, I've seen many players come and go. There is always a special quality about the outstanding ones. When Willie Mays broke in with the New York Giants in 1951, there was something about him that told all of us he would be great. Ted Williams, Joe DiMaggio, Mike Schmidt, Carl Yastrzemski, Pete Rose, Al Kaline, George Brett—all of them have that quality.

Nothing is more exciting than seeing the birth of a true baseball star and then being able to follow him throughout his career. Dan Schlossberg gives us a touch of that in his new book. Baseball couldn't find anybody better than Dan to do the job. So, enjoy Schlossberg's insights into the game he loves as you read his profiles of these modern baseball stars.

My boyhood heroes were of an earlier era—stars like Frankie Frisch, Charlie Gehringer, Hank Greenberg, Babe Ruth, and Ty Cobb. But these moderns loom just as large and just as impressively to their generation. They are the heroes today. They are the ones who can grab a headline and make it scream. And they are the ones whom Dan Schlossberg delineates so well for all of us.

Baseball thanks Dan Schlossberg for his devotion and his ability. Those qualities will shine through to you as you enjoy his profiles of today's greats of the game.

Ernie Harwell
Farmington Hills, Michigan

(Author's note: Ernie Harwell, voice of the Detroit Tigers since 1960, is the dean of American League broadcasters. He began announcing major league games in 1948, when the Brooklyn Dodgers traded a catcher to obtain his services from the Atlanta Crackers.

PREFACE

More than ten years have passed since Ray Robinson, the *Seventeen* magazine editor who moonlights as a baseball writer, asked me to write five profiles of current players for a paperback book he was putting together.

That book, the twenty-first in an annual series, also contained the work of William Barry Furlong, Arnold Hano, Larry Bortstein, and Robinson himself—but even these masters of sports literature weren't enough to keep the series going.

Baseball has undergone tumultuous changes in the ensuing decade, but one factor remains constant: you can't have a game without players.

This book is an attempt to show that those players have personalities as well as statistics, backgrounds as wide as the Kansas plains, histories that shape their futures. Even casual baseball fans will be intrigued with the evolution of baseball's teenaged strikeout king, who began pitching only after an early fling as an outfielder–third baseman; the American League's All-Star Game starter, a college All-American outfielder signed as a pitcher after a scout saw him pitch two mop-up innings; and the prominent fireballer whose former catcher says, "He has a million-dollar arm and a ten-cent head."

The hitters are here too—including two long-time stars who were also included in the last edition of the Ray Robinson book. Steve Garvey may have switched teams, but he's still an October hero, the man many managers rate as the most dangerous clutch hitter in the game. The most dangerous power hitter, and the man most feared by rival clubs, is another National League slugger, Philadelphia's Mike Schmidt. He too was in the 1975 book.

As both a fan and a writer, I'm glad Contemporary Books has decided to resurrect a good idea that has lain dormant too long. The new format, with expanded statistics and ample use of photographs, is far more appealing than the old, but the problem of player selection remains unchanged. It's simply impossible to include every deserving athlete.

Shari Lesser, the energetic editor who nursed this project to fruition, insisted that each of the 26 teams be represented by at least one player. That, of course, created a dilemma not unlike that faced by the All-Star team managers every year: by including one player from each team, some deserving players may be left out.

For example, the pages that follow contain four profiles of Detroit Tigers. No other team has that many players represented, but some observers will argue that four members of a World Championship team aren't enough. Certainly fans of All-Star catcher Lance Parrish and right-handed pitcher Dan Petry, an 18-game winner, will feel that way; neither is included.

Also missing, but certainly worthy of strong consideration, are Phil Niekro, Dwight Evans, Wade Boggs, Lloyd Moseby, Andre Thornton, Doyle Alexander, and Bill Caudill—plus such perennial favorites as George Brett and Reggie Jackson.

National League fans may also be miffed if they search for Pete Rose, Steve Carlton, Nolan Ryan, Andre Dawson, Bill Madlock, Pedro Guerrero, Gary Matthews, Bull Durham, or Dave Parker.

Not that those players aren't major stars—some even destined for Cooperstown—but they just didn't jive with the concept and the intent of this book. Some of them, undoubtedly, will surface in future editions.

The choices were not always easy; the selection of Fernando Valenzuela over fellow Dodger pitchers Alejandro Pena and Orel Hershiser was not based on statistics alone, but also on what Fernando means to his team—and has meant over the last few seasons. Even though he lost 17 games, tied for most in the majors a year ago, Valenzuela remains the unquestioned ace of the Los Angeles staff, the "stopper" Tommy Lasorda counts on when things get rough. It was simply the combination of a bad start and lack of offensive support that contributed to Fernando's disappointing won–lost ledger. He remains the best pitcher on a team that depends on pitching—and arguably the best lefthander in the National League.

There are young stars (Mike Witt, Ryne Sandberg, Mike Boddicker) and old (Garvey, Schmidt, Goose Gossage, Bruce Sutter), players from every team and every position—even the abhorrent designated hitter. They are at the top of their profession in 1985 and that is why they are included in this book. I hope you enjoy reading it as much as I did assembling it.

Dan Schlossberg
Passaic, New Jersey
November 1984

JOAQUIN ANDUJAR
FREE SPIRIT OF ST. LOUIS

CAREER RECORD											
YEAR	CLUB	W-L	ERA	G	CG	ShO	SV	IP	H	BB	SO
1970	Bradenton	3-5	4.17	12	4	1	0	82	86	56	88
1971	Souix Falls	4-7	6.36	19	4	0	0	75	61	63	82
1972	Three Rivers	7-6	3.54	22	6	2	0	112	87	73	101
1973	Indianapolis	2.5	9.00	11	0	0	0	40	42	45	23
	Three Rivers	5-2	1.98	10	4	0	0	59	38	38	39
1974	Indianapolis	8-8	3.57	33	2	1	2	111	85	93	92
1975	Three Rivers	4-8	4.06	18	1	1	0	62	57	40	44
1976	Houston	9-10	3.61	28	9	4	0	172	163	75	59
1977	Houston	11-8	3.68	26	4	1	0	159	149	64	69
1978	Houston	5-7	3.41	35	2	0	1	111	88	58	55
1979	Houston	12-12	3.43	46	8	0	4	194	168	88	77
1980	Houston	3-8	3.91	35	0	0	2	122	132	43	75
1981	Houston/St. Louis	8-4	4.10	20	1	0	0	79.0	85	23	37
1982	St. Louis	15-10	2.47	38	9	5	0	265.2	237	50	137
1983	St. Louis	6-16	4.16	39	5	2	1	225.0	215	75	125
1984	St. Louis	20-14	3.34	36	12	4	0	261.1	218	70	147

LEAGUE CHAMPIONSHIP SERIES RECORD											
YEAR	CLUB vs. OPP.	W-L	ERA	G	CG	ShO	SV	IP	H	BB	SO
1980	Houston vs. Philadelphia	0-0	0.00	1	0	0	1	1	0	1	0
1982	St. Louis vs. Atlanta	1-0	2.70	1	0	0	0	6.2	6	2	4

WORLD SERIES RECORD											
YEAR	CLUB vs. OPP.	W-L	ERA	G	CG	ShO	SV	IP	H	BB	SO
1982	St. Louis vs. Milwaukee	2-0	1.35	2	0	0	0	13.1	10	1	4

Joaquin Andujar is a superstitious sort. He once showered in full uniform so he could "wash the bad out of it." He often tells the batboy to fetch him a stick so he can clean out his spikes—whether they're muddy or not. And he believes poor luck was the key reason his record went from 6–16 in 1983 to 20–14 in 1984.

He also has rather unorthodox ideas about other things. His hitting, for example. He homered twice last season—both times off righthanded pitchers—but did it once batting lefthanded and once batting righthanded.

Though managers swear lefthanded hitters have a natural advantage against righthanded pitchers, the switch-hitting Andujar doesn't necessarily agree. He says he bats righthanded with the bases empty because he has more power as a righthanded hitter. He also bats righthanded when he intends to bunt or if he's facing a pitcher he doesn't know (the theory being that a pitched ball that hits him will strike the left shoulder and not damage Andujar's pitching shoulder). The star St. Louis righthander turns around to bat lefty only against righthanders he knows or if there are men on base.

Has Cardinal manager Whitey Herzog attempted to change him? "What the hell do I know?" he says. "I'm only the manager."

COLORFUL CHARACTER

At age 32, the 6-0, 180-pound Dominican definitely dances to the beat of a different drummer. But no other National League pitcher won 20 games last year and the Cardinals don't plan to mess with success.

Consider the almost-legendary Andujar quote-book.

- Asked about his chances to win the Cy Young Award, the pitcher replied, "I've already won it, but they're not going to give it to me. I've got to go to the moon and win 120 games. Then they'll give Cy Young on the moon."
- When he pitched in short sleeves on a 42-degree day, he said, "You can't worry if it's cold. You can't worry if it's hot. You only worry if you're sick because then, if you don't get well, you die."
- A lost pop-up at Wrigley Field, where no night games are played, brought another response worth remembering: "It's hard to see the ball in the daytime here."

For all his talk, Andujar is an excellent pitcher, though he acknowledges the presence of record-smashing reliever Bruce Sutter last year was a big help to him.

Even with Sutter around, Andujar worked $261\frac{1}{3}$ innings, most in the league, finished one behind league leader Mario Soto with 12 complete games, and tied Dodgers Orel Hershiser and Alejandro Pena for the most shutouts (4).

"I don't know many pitchers who go out every four or five days and not get hurt," he says. "If I'm pitching for you, you're not going to worry about me. I never have a sore arm. I can pitch in the bullpen. I can go out and pitch nine innings, and two days later I can pitch three or four in the bullpen. I don't go out at night. I don't go to discos. I don't even know where one is in St. Louis."

UNDERPAID ACE

Though he's now in his 10th season, Andujar earned only $300,000—a paltry sum by today's inflated standards—last year. That should change soon, even though the pitcher's chance to test the waters of free agency won't come until 1986. When he resigned with the Cards as a free agent pitcher in 1981, he waived his right for a second chance at free agency for five years.

Though the pitcher has no plans to leave St. Louis, he needs more money to take better care of 12 persons—members of his own family, including a grandfather—in the Dominican Republic.

Andujar's chances to make money beyond his Cardinal contract were hurt not only when he finished fourth in the Cy Young Award voting but also when he was bypassed for the National League All-Star squad—even though his 12 wins led the league at the time Philadelphia manager Paul Owens made his selections.

"Juan Marichal won 20 or 25 games for many years and never won the Cy Young," Andujar says of his countryman, the one-time Giants star who is now enshrined in Cooperstown. "I know why I can't win it, but I can't say."

More year-to-year consistency would be a great help, according to some observers. After reaching the majors with the Houston Astros in 1976, Andujar has managed to put together a string of alternating good and bad years—except for the 1981–82 seasons with St. Louis.

"I'm not as bad as I was in 1983, but I'm not going to say I'm great either," says the veteran righthander. "I've been to two All-Star games. It surprises me if I pitch bad.

"When your record is 6–16, though, people make a big deal out of it. I just didn't pitch that poorly. If I had, my earned run average would have been twice as high as it was."

Andujar makes sense with that analysis; his 4.16 mark of 1983 was quite similar to the 4.10 mark he posted during the strike-torn 1981 campaign, when he won eight of 12 decisions in a season divided between Houston and St. Louis. But it can't compare with his career-best 2.47—second in the National League—of 1982, or even his 3.34 of last summer.

CHANGEUP HELPS

The difference for Andujar, in addition to better control, was a new-found changeup, making his usual assortment of fastballs and sliders more effective by keeping batters off balance.

"The changeup makes my fastball faster," says Andujar, who also credits Hub Kittle and Mike Roarke, St. Louis pitching coaches the last two seasons, for speeding his transition into a 20-game winner.

"Hub Kittle taught me everything I know," the pitcher insists, "but Mike Roarke helped me, too. I also enjoyed working with Tom Nieto, the catcher who came up last year. He calls a good game because he moves around. A catcher has to move to the inside corner and the outside corner. I don't like the catcher right down the middle of home plate, because then you're going to get killed."

As in 1983, Andujar began the year with a shutout. He lost his second outing of '84—he won his second straight in '83 before losing 16 of 20 decisions the rest of the way—but then proceeded to take command. He was outstanding in eight of his first nine starts and, at one stretch, posted a 1.98 earned run average over $59\frac{2}{3}$ innings.

He was NL Player of the Week for the period of May 14–20 when he pitched two complete-game victories, both eight-hitters, fanned 10, walked only one, and connected for his first major-league grand slam (off Atlanta's Jeff Dedmon). Andujar even called the shot; while in the on-deck circle, he pointed to the right-field wall and told George Hendrick and Tito Landrum he was going to hit a home run.

He also learned from one particularly bad outing—seven runs in three innings at San Diego. "I tried to throw everything hard, right down the middle," he said later. "That's how I tried to pitch in 1983."

Unrattled by the poor performance, Andujar went on to become the first Cardinal 20-game winner since Bob Forsch in 1977 and only the second Dominican (Juan Marichal was the other) to reach the magic circle, though Mario Soto and Pascual Perez are strong candidates to join them.

"He'll tell you his luck is changing," says Whitey Herzog, "but I'll tell you he's pitching better and that's why his luck is changing."

Joaquin Andujar was the National League's only 20-game winner in 1984

TONY ARMAS
BOSTON BOMBER

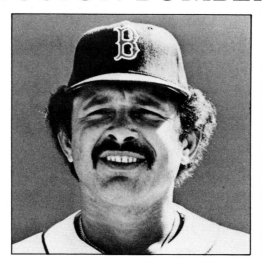

		CAREER RECORD									
YEAR	CLUB	AVG.	G	AB	R	H	2B	3B	HR	RBI	SB
1971	Bradenton	.231	43	169	12	39	3	3	0	17	2
	Monroe	.227	31	88	7	20	3	3	1	10	1
1972	Gastonia	.266	117	399	50	106	18	4	9	51	11
1973	Sherbrooke	.301	84	302	26	91	15	5	11	45	5
1974	Thetford Mines	.277	137*	476	64	132	26	3	15	81	10
1975	Charleston	.300	128	450	65	135	28	4	12	72	6
1976	Charleston	.235	114	409	62	96	24	1	21	67	7
	Pittsburgh	.333	4	6	0	2	0	0	0	1	0
1977	Oakland	.240	118	363	26	87	8	2	13	53	1
1978	Oakland	.213	91	239	17	51	6	1	2	13	1
1979	Oakland	.248	80	278	29	69	9	3	11	34	1
1980	Oakland	.279	158	628	87	175	18	8	35	109	5
1981	Oakland	.261	109	440	51	115	24	3	22	76	5
1982	Oakland	.233	138	536	58	125	19	2	28	89	2
1983	Boston	.218	145	574	77	125	23	2	36	107	0
1984	Boston	.268	157	639	107	171	29	5	43	123	1

*—Led league

		DIVISION SERIES RECORD									
YEAR	CLUB vs. OPP.	AVG.	G	AB	R	H	2B	3B	HR	RBI	SB
1981	Oakland vs. Kansas City	.545	3	11	1	6	2	0	0	3	0

		CHAMPIONSHIP SERIES RECORD									
YEAR	CLUB vs. OPP.	AVG.	G	AB	R	H	2B	3B	HR	RBI	SB
1981	Oakland vs. New York	.167	3	12	0	2	0	0	0	0	0

Tony Armas must be wondering what he has to do to get the recognition he deserves.

He was a major star for three of the six seasons he spent with the Oakland Athletics, but was overshadowed by Rickey Henderson's base-stealing, Billy Martin's brash managerial style, and the antics of unpredictable owner Charles O. Finley.

Traded to Boston in December 1982, Armas found the Fenway Park fans concerned first with retiring legend Carl Yastrzemski, second with continuing legend Jim Rice, and third with the front-office ownership tussle that threatened to tear the team apart.

The Venezuelan star simply went about his business: hitting long home runs, knocking in runs, and utilizing a powerful right arm to throttle enemy runners on the basepaths.

UNSUNG HERO

Even league leadership in home runs and runs

batted in didn't remove the cloak of anonymity. Armas led the majors with 43 home runs and 123 runs batted in and teamed with Dwight Evans, who hit 32 round-trippers, to form baseball's most potent 1-2 punch. Nobody seemed to notice—even though the Red Sox became the third team in baseball history to have three 100-RBI outfielders in the same season (the 1921 Detroit Tigers had Harry Heilmann, Ty Cobb, and Bobby Veach, while the 1929 Chicago Cubs had Briggs Stephenson, Hack Wilson, and Kiki Cuyler).

Together with Jim Rice, who finished one RBI behind his league-leading teammate, sluggers Evans and Armas, hitting behind .325 hitter Wade Boggs, were the key reasons the Red Sox led the majors with a .283 batting average and ranked just behind Detroit in runs scored.

Armas credits hitting coach Walt Hriniak for his excellent showing.

"I was embarrassed when I hit .218 in 1983— even though I had 31 homers and 107 RBI," concedes the leading Venezuelan in the major leagues. "During spring training, I worked with Walter on trying to hit the ball up the middle and toward right field. The year before, I was trying to pull everything out of the park. I don't do that anymore unless it's the late innings and we're tied or behind by a run."

Armas, who marks his 32nd birthday around All-Star time, made the American League squad for the second time last year but was left in the on-deck circle when Rickey Henderson, his former Oakland teammate, fanned to end the game with a runner on second. Had he come to the plate, Armas might have represented the potential tying run, since the National League took a 3-1 victory in the Candlestick Park contest.

Tony Armas teamed with Jim Rice and Dwight Evans to make the Boston Red Sox the third club in baseball history to have three 100-RBI outfielders.

PHYSICAL PROBLEMS

The 6-1, 192-pound righthanded hitter started slowly because of off-season elbow surgery that led to shoulder problems. Armas had a .242 average and eight homers in mid-May but was up to 22 home runs and 63 RBI by the All-Star break. One factor that helped a lot was the May 25 acquisition of Bill Buckner from the Chicago Cubs.

"That made a big difference," explains Armas, who broke into the pros as a Pittsburgh Pirates' farmhand in 1971. "Before, they were kind of pitching around me. After we got Buckner, they couldn't. I got a lot better pitches to hit."

Armas opened the season batting third, ahead of Jim Rice, but the two switched positions in May as Ralph Houk, then Red Sox manager, tried

a shake-well plan in an effort to generate more offense. Both hitters responded and the team revived after a lethargic getaway. Having Mike Easler and later Buckner behind them also helped.

Armas, who still plays winter ball in Caracas, is one of 14 children (10 brothers and three sisters) and remembers trying times from his youth. Now, he helps those less fortunate than he—by buying 2500 Red Sox tickets and distributing them through the Boys Club and Girls Club of Boston. He also has three children of his own.

The handsome Latin slugger has brought smiles to the youth of Fenway since his arrival from Oakland in the five-man trade that sent Carney Lansford to the Bay Area. Armas willingly moved from right field, his position with the

Athletics, to center, where he hadn't played since 1977, and showed the same strong arm that had him ranked with Evans as the best-throwing right-fielders in the league. He excelled at drifting back on long flies, sealed the gaps to his left and right, and used his speed to cover considerable ground between Evans and Rice.

ACHILLES HEEL

While his defense leaves little to be desired, the same cannot be said about the offensive contributions of Tony Armas. He's struck out at least 115 times in each of the last four seasons (including the strike-shortened 1981 campaign), he has a tendency to swing at bad balls rather than wait out a walk (he got only 32 free passes last year), and he tries to pull so many pitches that he hits into a large number of double-plays.

On the plus side, he's had three seasons of at least 35 homers and 105 RBI and is coming off a season in which his batting average rose 50 points, proving the value of proper coaching. Armas finished with a flourish—hammering home runs Nos. 40, 41, and 42 in Baltimore on the next-to-last weekend of the season and No. 43 before the closing bell. No other major-leaguer reached the 40-homer plateau last summer.

Only 11 active players have had 40-homer seasons and only three of them—Mike Schmidt, George Foster, and Reggie Jackson—have done it more than once.

"When you discuss a power prospect now, scouts say he has '30–35 potential,' " says White Sox general manager Roland Hemond. "Years ago, the same scout would say '40–45 power' if he wanted to get your attention. Today you hardly hear anyone talk about 40 homers. The new parks are bigger and have deeper alleys."

TOUGH PARKS

Armas admits Yankee Stadium, Royals Stadium, and Oakland-Alameda County Stadium are three of the tougher home run parks for him, but realizes how fortunate he is to play half his home games in Fenway Park, with the Green Monster—the towering left field wall—a scant 315 feet from home plate. It's a match made in heaven.

That wall helped Armas compile a 19-game hitting streak, his career high, early in the campaign. He went on to join teammates Rice, Evans, and Easler as Red Sox who amassed more than 300 total bases in 1984 (the entire National League had just three players at that level).

"It's tough for a manager to play percentage when these guys are up," Ralph Houk admitted at midseason. "Do you walk Boggs to pitch to Evans? Do you walk Evans to pitch to Rice? Do you walk Rice to pitch to Armas? Do you walk Armas to pitch to Easler or Easler to pitch to Buckner? I'm glad I don't have to make those decisions."

Thanks to the overload of sluggers, the Red Sox paced the American League with 1,598 hits, 2,490 total bases, and a .441 slugging percentage. Tony Armas was a big factor in all three areas—and figures to continue in that role for years to come. If he maintains his health, continues the coaching sessions with Walt Hriniak, and benefits from the booming bats behind him in the batting order, he's a logical bet to become the first 50-homer hitter since George Foster hit 52 for the 1977 Reds. No one in Boston is betting against him.

HAROLD BAINES
CHICAGO'S QUIET CLOUTER

CAREER RECORD													
YEAR	CLUB	AVG.	G	AB	R	H	2B	3B	HR	RBI	BB	SO	SB
1977	Appleton	.261	69	222	37	56	11	2	5	29	36	62	2
1978	Knoxville	.275	137	502	70	138	16	6	13	72	43	91	3
1979	Iowa	.298	125	466	87	139	25	8	22	87	33	80	5
1980	Chicago, AL	.255	141	491	55	125	23	6	13	49	19	65	2
1981	Chicago, AL	.286	82	280	42	80	11	7	10	41	12	41	6
1982	Chicago, AL	.271	161	608	89	165	29	8	25	105	49	95	10
1983	Chicago, AL	.280	156	596	76	167	32	3	20	99	49	85	7
1984	Chicago, AL	.304	147	569	72	173	28	10	29	94			1

LEAGUE CHAMPIONSHIP SERIES RECORD										
YEAR	CLUB vs. OPP.	AVG.	G	AB	R	H	2B	3B	HR	RBI	SB
1983	Chicago vs. Baltimore	.125	4	16	0	2	0	0	2	0	0

On May 9, 1984, Harold Baines hit a home run.

That wasn't so unusual for a man who would finish the season with 29, but the timing of the blast was most unusual. It came in the 25th inning of a game originally started on May 8 but suspended after 17 innings because of an American League rule that prohibits a new inning from starting after 12:59 A.M.

The Baines home run, on a 2-and-0 count from Milwaukee Brewers' righthander Chuck Porter, traveled 420 feet into the Comiskey Park bullpen, giving the Chicago White Sox a 7–6 victory. Never has a home run been hit in such a late inning; never has a game exceeded eight hours from start to finish (this one took 8:06); and never has an American League contest consumed so many innings (two National League clubs, the Brooklyn Dodgers and Boston Braves, played to a 1–1 tie in 26 innings in 1920).

The heroic hit, which gave Tom Seaver a rare relief win (in the seventh bullpen outing of his 17-year career), was only Baines's second in 20 at-bats and his first homer in more than a month.

Though neither Baines nor the White Sox realized it at the time, the 25th-inning home run set the stage for an outstanding season by the Chicago rightfielder—despite his usual slow start.

With the slugger's average mired at .129 in the early going, manager Tony LaRussa, the Job of the dugout set, gave the star a vote of confidence.

"Harold has shown more discipline at the plate at this point in the season than he ever has in the past," the pilot pointed out. "I'd venture to say that if he keeps swinging the way he has, he'll have his best season."

HOT BAT

The 25-year-old lefthanded hitter caught fire as the weather warmed and, by season's end, had more than justified his manager's judgment. His .541 slugging percentage led the American League and he ranked sixth in the circuit with 67 extra-base hits and 308 total bases—single-season power production exceeded only twice previously in White Sox history (Joe Jackson had 336 total bases in 1920 and Carl Reynolds had 329 in 1930).

The first member of the White Sox to reach double figures in doubles, triples, and home runs since Jorge Orta did it in 1975, Baines led the club with 94 runs batted in and a .304 batting average—the first .300 performance of his five-year career. One of four Sox with 20 home runs, he now has 97 lifetime, tying Pete Ward for fourth on the Chicago career list but leading all left-handed hitters in club history. In the past three seasons, he's averaged 99 RBI.

"I just do the same basic things," says the soft-spoken slugger. "I see the ball and try to hit it hard somewhere."

The statistics bear him out; from May 25 until mid-August, he lifted his average from the sub-.200 doldrums with a .373 streak. He was American League Player-of-the-Week for the period of August 5–12, when he had a .448 batting average, 1.069 slugging percentage, and four home runs—including two game-winners.

Harold Baines is big on game-winning RBI; in 1983, he plated 22 of them, surpassing the previous major-league mark shared by Don Baylor, Jack Clark, and Keith Hernandez.

Last year, a hefty percentage of his game-winners were home runs; through August 9, eight of nine Baines home runs had won games.

Twice, Baines has hit three home runs in a game—most recently on September 18, 1984, against the Minnesota Twins. In that game, he hit solo homers to right in the first and fifth and a two-run, 460-foot homer to right center in the seventh.

BIG NIGHT

On July 7, 1982, Baines was even more productive. His three-homer display against Detroit at Comiskey Park that night included an eighth-inning grand slam against Elias Sosa.

"That was a little more enjoyable," remembers Baines, who went on to enjoy his lone 100-RBI campaign that summer. "I'm supposed to hit home runs and knock in runs. That's why I'm here."

Actually, Baines wears a Chicago uniform because the Sox made him the first player chosen in the June 1977 draft of amateur free agents. Three years later, he had reached the major leagues to stay.

The 6-2, 189-pound slugger earns $500,000 per year in a contract that runs through this season, with three option years attached at the club's discretion. When he signed the original three-year deal at the end of the 1982 campaign, the figures seemed overly generous for a player with relatively little experience. By today's market standards, however, it is likely that the contract will have to be upgraded before it runs out.

Baines won't make a whole lot of noise about it; that's not his style.

"He values his privacy, including his comments," LaRussa says. "But he shows his emotions more than he used to. To do what Harold does, the fire has got to be burning very brightly, whether anyone can see it or not."

The White Sox pilot got a scare last summer when Baines, posing for a pregame picture, was struck in the head by an errant pepper game liner hit by Tom Seaver. With the star complaining of a headache, LaRussa scratched him from the lineup—reluctantly.

"I have never yet had a game that Harold has not played in where I felt comfortable," he said at the time.

Baines, selected over Paul Molitor and Terry Kennedy in the amateur draft, was actually scouted by Bill Veeck, two-time White Sox owner, as a 12-year-old Little Leaguer on Maryland's Eastern Shore.

VEECK CONNECTION

There was considerable criticism of his selection because of the "Veeck connection," but Baines has silenced the skeptics with his smoking bat. Even in the minors, he gave hint of things to come when he homered twice in an inning for Chicago's Triple-A Iowa affiliate on August 4, 1979. Three years later, he became the youngest player in White Sox history to collect 100 RBI in a season.

The rifle-armed rightfielder, a native of Easton, Maryland who makes his current home in St. Michaels, Maryland with wife Maria, Baines has cultivated a well-deserved reputation as one of the game's premier clutch hitters. In 1984, when the Sox slipped from champions of the West to a fifth-place finish, 10 games behind front-running Kansas City, Baines still managed to collect 17 game-winning hits, tied with Kirk Gibson and Jim Rice for second in the league (Eddie Murray had 19).

It's no surprise he does so well; a free swinger and first-ball hitter with good power to the opposite field, Baines rarely walks, even if that means he must chase breaking balls out of the strike zone. A streak hitter who once hit three grand-slams in a week, the Chisox stalwart does have occasional slumps but never lets them interfere with his even temperament.

"There's no limit to his potential," says Kansas City broadcaster Denny Matthews. "He's one of the coming young stars of the game. In recent years, he's become bigger and stronger. If he learns to be more selective at the plate and hits for a higher average, he'll really be something special."

The White Sox think he already is.

BUDDY BELL
TOPS AT THIRD

		CAREER RECORD										
YEAR	CLUB	AVG.	G	AB	R	H	2B	3B	HR	RBI	SB
1969	Sarasota	.229	51	170	18	39	4	3	3	24	3
1970	Sumter	.265	121	442	81	117	19	3	12	75	9
1971	Wichita	.289	129	470	65	136	23	1	11	59	7
1972	Cleveland	.255	132	466	49	119	21	1	9	36	6
1973	Cleveland	.268	156	631	86	169	23	7	14	59	7
1974	Cleveland	.262	116	423	51	111	15	1	7	46	1
1975	Cleveland	.271	153	553	66	150	20	4	10	59	6
1976	Cleveland	.281	159	604	75	170	26	2	7	60	3
1977	Cleveland	.292	129	479	64	140	23	4	11	64	1
1978	Cleveland	.282	142	556	71	157	27	8	6	62	1
1979	Texas	.299	162	670	89	200	42	3	18	101	5
1980	Texas	.329	129	490	76	161	24	4	17	83	3
1981	Texas	.294	97	360	44	106	16	1	10	64	3
1982	Texas	.296	148	537	62	159	27	2	13	67	5
1983	Texas	.277	156	618	75	171	35	3	14	66	3
1984	Texas	.315	148	553	88	174	36	5	11	83	2

Though third base is generally considered to be a position for a power hitter, the man generally regarded as the best third baseman in baseball has played 13 years without a single 20-home run campaign.

In fact, Buddy Bell—unlike his slugging father—has had four seasons when his home run total didn't even go to double-figures.

Like Brooks Robinson, the long-time Baltimore Orioles' star who is now a member of the Baseball Hall of Fame, Buddy Bell is known more for his play around third base than his abilities in the batters' box.

"Defensively, he's a combination of Graig Nettles and Aurelio Rodriguez," suggests former teammate Jim Kern, a once-intimidating relief pitcher trying to recapture his old form. "Buddy has Nettles's reactions and range and Rodriguez's arm."

He also has the endorsement of a hard-to-please authority, Texas manager Doug Rader.

"To catch a ball properly," says Rader, a former good-hit, good-field third baseman, mostly with the Houston Astros, "you need good feet. If you don't get yourself in position to catch properly, you won't do it. Buddy doesn't have foot speed, but he's got excellent agility for a third baseman."

PERENNIAL STAR

A five-time All-Star, the 6-2, 185-pound Bell enjoyed his second .300 season last year, when his .315 led the club and ranked fourth in the American League. He had 83 runs batted in—second on the team and an amazing figure for a hitter with only 11 home runs—and 10 of those RBI were game winners, one behind team leader Larry Parrish.

It is ironic that Parrish, whose 22 homers and 101 RBI led the club, spent the year as a combination rightfielder and designated hitter while Bell anchored third base for the sixth straight year since his acquisition from Cleveland.

Parrish, like Bell, is a third baseman by trade. But Bell's presence at the position precluded the Rangers from placing Parrish there; he was assigned to outfield duty during his first Texas spring training camp in 1982. That was no knock on Parrish, but a tribute to Bell, who has now won Gold Gloves in all six of his Texas seasons.

No less an authority than George Brett calls Bell the league's top all-around player, while Detroit manager Sparky Anderson is on record as rating Bell above anyone in either league. Rader's words are simpler: "He's the dream player of every manager in this game."

Partly to quiet persistent rumors that the talent-poor Rangers will trade their star attraction for a package of prospects, Rader named Bell Texas captain last year. At the time of the appointment, the manager noted that the third baseman performs valuable off-the-field duties never noticed by fans or media.

SOLID CITIZEN

"He's performed a tremendous service to me by keeping things smoothed out in the clubhouse," revealed Rader, well-aware that keeping discipline on a cellar-dwelling team is difficult at best. "It's important for other organizations to know how we feel about Buddy."

It still boggles the mind to realize that the Rangers acquired Bell from Cleveland in an even-up swap for the much-maligned Toby Harrah on December 8, 1978. Bell, who won't turn 34 until late August, is three years younger and vastly more talented than Harrah, who finished last season riding the bench for the New York Yankees.

Bell took a .284 lifetime batting average into the 1984 campaign, though that average might have been considerably higher had he been able to bat against his own pitching staffs in Cleveland and Texas. Playing for consistently bad teams has cloaked Bell in anonymity, while playing half his games in Arlington Stadium, a hitter's nightmare, has distorted his statistics.

"You have to be optimistic," Bell admits. "If the club shows patience with what we've got, we could have a gold mine."

Good infield prospects keep popping up—Curtis Wilkerson and Jeff Kunkel to name two—and the 1984 addition of Gary Ward was a major factor in the revival of the Rangers' offense, but the club still hit bottom in the American League West with a 69–92 record, 14½ games behind the front-running Kansas City Royals.

Would Texas trade him in an effort to narrow that deficit?

According to owner Eddie Chiles, "Buddy Bell

Buddy Bell, whose .315 batting average ranked fourth in the American League last year, has been an All-Star five times. The slick-fielding third baseman of the Texas Rangers has been the trade target of many envious rivals.

comes about as close to being untouchable as anybody in Ranger baseball, including me. We might trade him for the whole Dodger pitching staff, but that would be about it."

The 1984 rumor mill had second baseman Steve Sax and righthanded starting pitcher Bob Welch going from Los Angeles to Texas in exchange for Bell.

TRADE TALK

More than half the teams in baseball have inquired about Bell within the last two seasons, club officials admit, but hard offers have been scarce—apparently because other teams know it would take a monumental package to pry Bell loose.

The annual rumors annoy Bell but provide Hot Stove League fodder for the infielder and his family: wife Gloria, three sons, and a daughter. They live in Cincinnati, the same town where father Gus found stardom as a slugging outfielder for the Reds.

"A father can do only so much," says Gus, who hit 206 homers in a 15-year career that also included tours with the Pirates, Mets, and Braves from 1950 to 1964. "Buddy made it because of his desire."

The Bells, whose nine combined All-Star appearances lead all father-and-son combinations, remain a close family; Gus still works in Cincinnati, as a sales manager for a temporary-help service.

"I never wanted to do anything but be an athlete," insists Buddy. "More than anything, I enjoy the fun. It's not so much on the field, but before and after the game. We're still kids. People come off the street and ask themselves, 'Are those guys 30 or 10?' You should stay as young as you can for as long as you can."

Originally a second baseman, Buddy Bell was signed by Cleveland after the Indians selected negotiating rights to him in the 16th round of the 1969 amateur free agent draft. He broke in with Sarasota, Florida, in 1969, three years before he reached the American League to stay—as a combination outfielder-third baseman. He's also played some shortstop in the major leagues and had a taste of first base to boot.

SLICK FIELDER

Despite knee and back problems in recent years, he remains in a class by himself as a defensive third baseman—with excellent hands, fine arm, and above-average reactions. A better-fielding shortstop (maybe Kunkel will be ready this year) would enable him to play a step closer to the third base line, where he would be even more effective as a modern-day Hoover at the hot corner.

Insiders insist Bell is almost as consistent at bat as he is on the field. He seldom strikes out or finds himself embroiled in lengthy slumps. An excellent hit-and-run man who usually bats near the top of the lineup, Bell has a quick bat, good knowledge of the strike zone, and the ability to hit the ball to all fields. In Texas, such technique is the most logical route to batting success.

"I'm probably one of the least scientific players of all time," he says. "If you think too much you make the game too complicated. You hit the ball and catch the ball and that's about it."

Buddy Bell does both of those things very well.

BERT BLYLEVEN
WINNING PITCHER, LOSING TEAM

| | CAREER RECORD | | | | | | | | | | |
YEAR	CLUB	W-L	ERA	G	CG	ShO	SV	IP	H	BB	SO
1969	Sarasota	2-2	2.81	7	1	1	1	32	31	11	39
	Orlando	5-0	1.46	6	5	1	0	37	26	14	41
1970	Evansville	4-2	2.50	8	2	1	0	54	48	12	63
	Minnesota	10-9	3.18	27	5	1	0	164	143	47	135
1971	Minnesota	16-15	2.82	38	17	5	0	278	267	59	224
1972	Minnesota	17-17	2.73	39	11	3	0	287	247	69	228
1973	Minnesota	20-17	2.52	40	25	9	0	325	296	67	258
1974	Minnesota	17-17	2.66	37	19	3	0	281	244	77	249
1975	Minnesota	15-10	3.00	35	20	3	0	276	219	84	233
1976	Minnesota	4-5	3.13	12	4	0	0	95	101	35	75
	Texas	9-11	2.76	24	14	6	0	202	182	46	144
1977	Texas	14-12	2.72	30	15	5	0	235	181	69	182
1978	Pittsburgh	14-10	3.02	34	11	4	0	244	217	66	182
1979	Pittsburgh	12-5	3.61	37	4	0	0	237	238	92	172
1980	Pittsburgh	8-13	3.82	32	5	2	0	217	219	59	168
1981	Cleveland	11-7	2.88	20	9	1	0	159	145	40	107
1982	Cleveland	2-2	4.87	4	0	0	0	20.1	16	11	19
1983	Cleveland	7-10	3.91	24	5	0	0	156.1	160	44	123
1984	Cleveland	19-7	2.87	33	12	4	0	245	204	74	170

| | LEAGUE CHAMPIONSHIP SERIES RECORD | | | | | | | | | | |
YEAR	CLUB vs. OPP.	W-L	ERA	G	GS	CG	ShO	SV	IP	H	BB	SO
1970	Minnesota vs. Baltimore	0-0	0.00	1	0	0	0	0	2	2	0	2
1979	Pittsburgh vs. Cincinnati	1-0	1.00	1	1	1	0	0	9	8	0	9

| | WORLD SERIES RECORD | | | | | | | | | | |
YEAR	CLUB vs. OPP.	W-L	ERA	G	GS	CG	ShO	SV	IP	H	BB	SO
1979	Pittsburgh vs. Baltimore	1-0	1.80	2	1	0	0	0	10	8	3	4

Rick Sutcliffe, winner of the National League's Cy Young Award for pitching excellence, feels Bert Blyleven, his former teammate at Cleveland, should have won the American League honor last year.

"I know how hard it is to pitch in Cleveland, when you're out of the pennant race in May and nobody's there to cheer you on," says Sutcliffe, who copped the NL citation only after Cleveland traded him to the Chicago Cubs in June. "Bert definitely deserves it in the American League. But I'll tell you something else—if somebody had come up to me at the end of May and told me Bert Blyleven and I would be contending for the Cy

Bert Blyleven has been an established big-league pitcher since 1970. Though he has never thrown a no-hitter in the majors, he has limited rival clubs to one hit in a game on five different occasions.

Young Award at the end of the 1984 season, I would have recommended a very good psychiatrist."

Like Sutcliffe, who lost five of nine decisions for Cleveland before his trade on June 13, Blyleven did not start the year like a house on fire. But a 15–4 record over his last 22 starts gave him a season's log of 19–7 for a team that finished 12 games under .500 and 29 games out of first place.

He tied Jack Morris for second in victories (Mike Boddicker had one more) and ranked second in the league with his .731 winning percentage. His 2.86 earned run average placed third and he also forged a third-place tie by throwing four shutouts. Blyleven finished fourth in the league with 12 complete games and 170 strikeouts.

TOUGH YEAR

Those statistics would make most men happy, but the 6-3, 205-pound righthander described the season as frustrating.

"I have to concentrate more on personal goals than team goals," he said late in the year. "I'm not 23 and trying to prove I can pitch in the big leagues. At 33, your main concern is being on a winning club. Maybe that's why our players are a little more aggressive when I pitch.

"I demand a lot from myself and I demand a lot from the guys playing behind me. They are going to get the best I have to offer and I expect to get the best from my teammates. Sometimes I try to say little things to get them motivated. I shouldn't have to do that, but that's what happens on a team that isn't going anywhere."

Blyleven repeatedly asked to be traded during the 1984 campaign but also insisted he would make a maximum effort wherever he pitched.

"Anybody would be foolish not to want to play for a contender," he said, "but I still will go out and give 100 percent no matter what team I pitch for."

Blyleven, who broke into pro ball in 1969 and advanced to the Minnesota Twins the following year, probably would have led the American League in victories last year if not for injury. He won four of his first six decisions, then fractured a bone on the outside of his right foot, forcing his placement on the disabled list May 23. The break, which resulted when the pitcher stepped on a loose outfield ball while shagging flies, forced Blyleven to miss six starts. Had he won two of those six, with everything else remaining equal, Blyleven would have fashioned his second 20-win season and would have won one more game than the league's lone 10-game winner, Mike Boddicker.

INJURY JINX

The veteran curveball master, who has also played for Texas and Pittsburgh, has spent much of his Cleveland career on the injured list. After an 11–7 debut with the Tribe in 1981, Blyleven suffered a severe muscle tear in his elbow in May and, needing surgical repair, was lost for the season. A sciatic nerve problem and subsequent shoulder injury killed most of his 1983 campaign.

Memories of those injuries aroused the ire of Cleveland president Gabe Paul when Blyleven asked to be traded last year. "After paying him for two years of nonproductivity, we figure he owes us something," Paul said. "The trade request is unreasonable at a time when he finally can produce for a team that is paying him a damn good salary. He owes some loyalty to the club and to the City of Cleveland."

Blyleven's salary of $650,000—more than double what the Cardinals paid 20-game winner Joaquin Andujar last year—was fair by current standards, but several pitchers with less ability earn more in other cities.

"I'm sorry I got hurt," the pitcher said. "I'm not a pitching machine, and even they break down. I couldn't predict I'd hurt my elbow and have an operation. And I couldn't predict I'd hurt my shoulder when I tried to come back too soon."

When a clubhouse prankster changed his locker stall nameplate to CRYLEVEN, the media reported it—adding to the strain between player and management.

"The Cryleven stuff started in Pittsburgh," the pitcher said. "I was unhappy there because of the way I was used, so I complained about it."

Blyleven had few complaints under Pat Corrales last year. A model of consistency, he went at least seven innings in 26 of his 32 starts and allowed three runs or less 22 times. Cleveland scored just six runs in his seven losses.

On July 13, he one-hit Texas—the fifth time he has limited the opposition to one hit in a game—and he also tossed two two-hitters. For some reason, Blyleven was at his best against one of the best clubs—the champion Kansas City Royals of the American League West. He went 4–0 with a 1.44 ERA against Kaycee to move one ahead of the retired Jim Palmer, whose 20 lifetime wins against the Royals previously led the league.

CONSISTENT CAMPAIGN

Only in September did Blyleven lose more than one game (he dropped a pair of 4–1 decisions in the final month) as he fashioned the first 19-win season by a Cleveland pitcher since Len Barker, now with Atlanta, went 19–12 in 1980. Blyleven himself had not won as many games in a season since 1973, when he enjoyed his lone 20-win campaign with a 20–17 log for Minnesota.

He got his 19th win on the last day of the season with a 7–4 win over the Twins—the team that got him into professional baseball. Blyleven was Minnesota's Number 3 selection in the regular phase of the amateur free agent draft in June 1969.

Though he has pitched for a string of bad ball clubs, Blyleven has been a pillar of effectiveness; he has a lifetime American League earned run

Blyleven's curveball helped him post a 19–7 record for the also-ran Indians last year.

average of 2.88 and an NL mark of 3.47, which combines to a neat 3.00 earned runs per nine innings over 15 seasons.

While he is regarded as baseball's best curveball specialist, Blyleven says there are hitters who can adjust to his sweeping roundhouse pitch. The five best, he reveals, are Robin Yount, Cal Ripken, Cliff Johnson, Buddy Bell, and Mickey Hatcher.

Unfortunately, Blyleven occasionally throws a curve at a teammate. Early last season, after a pop fly fell between second baseman Tony Bernazard and rightfielder George Vukovich—resulting in two earned runs because it was scored a hit—the pitcher protested to the official scorer. Blyleven, trying to protect his ERA, pointed out that Vukovich had touched the ball.

When the scorer refused to change his decision, Blyleven phoned the American League office in New York in an attempt to go over his head. That didn't work either but if it had, Bert Blyleven and not Mike Boddicker would have been the American League leader in earned run average in 1984.

Even though he wasn't, no one can detract from Blyleven's fine season.

16

MIKE BODDICKER
BELATED BELLWETHER IN BALTIMORE

CAREER RECORD

YEAR	CLUB	W-L	ERA	G	CG	ShO	SV	IP	H	BB	SO
1976	Bluefield	2-1	0.47	8	0	0	2	19	9	10	28
	Charlotte	4-3	1.94	10	5	2	0	65	42	17	48
	Rochester	1-0	1.80	1	0	0	0	5	4	2	3
1979	Charlotte	9-3	3.00	14	8	2	0	102	82	36	89
	Rochester	4-6	6.00	15	2	1	0	72	88	27	48
1980	Rochester	12-9	2.18	25	13	4	0	190	149	35	109
	Baltimore	0-1	6.43	1	0	0	0	7	6	5	4
1981	Rochester	10-10	4.20	30	8	3	0	182	182	66	109
	Baltimore	0-0	4.50	2	0	0	0	6	6	2	2
1982	Rochester	10-5	3.58	20	5	1	0	133.1	121	36	82
	Baltimore	1-0	3.51	7	0	0	0	25.2	25	12	20
1983	Rochester	3-1	1.90	4	1	1	0	23.2	17	13	18
	Baltimore	16-8	2.77	24	10	5	0	179.0	141	52	120
1984	Baltimore	20-11	2.79	34	16	4	0	261.1	218	81	128

—Led league

LEAGUE CHAMPIONSHIP SERIES RECORD

YEAR	CLUB vs. OPP.	W-L	ERA	G	CG	ShO	SV	IP	H	BB	SO
1983	Baltimore vs. Chicago	1-0	0.00	1	1	1	0	9	5	3	14

WORLD SERIES RECORD

YEAR	CLUB vs. OPP.	W-L	ERA	G	CG	ShO	SV	IP	H	BB	SO
1983	Baltimore vs. Philadelphia	1-0	0.00	1	1	0	0	9	3	0	6

The Baltimore Orioles—a team reputed to know pitching talent—had Mike Boddicker on a yo-yo for six years. Signed by the Birds after his sixth-round selection in the June 1978 draft of amateur free agents, Boddicker pitched for at least two teams per season from 1978, his first professional season, through 1983.

He spent parts of all six years in Rochester, New York, home of Baltimore's Triple-A affiliate, and got so fed up with his earthbound answer to the space shuttle that he seriously considered the possibility of pitching for another organization.

That might have happened in 1983, when his May 5 recall exhausted his minor league options. The Orioles had to keep him or return him to the minors as a "frozen" player, eligible to be plucked from the Rochester roster in the annual winter draft.

Making that decision wasn't easy—especially since Boddicker had failed to convince long-time

Oriole pilot Earl Weaver that he could pitch on the big league level—but Joe Altobelli, Weaver's successor, needed pitching so badly that he gave the much maligned righthander a chance.

On May 8, the pitcher threw a scoreless inning-and-two-thirds against the Oakland Athletics. Nine days later, in his second major league start, Boddicker bamboozled the Chicago White Sox, tossing a 5–0 five-hitter for the first complete game of his big league career. With veteran starter Mike Flanagan out for three months with a knee injury suffered in the opener of that May 17 doubleheader, Boddicker's timing was propitious; Altobelli announced that the rookie had won a spot in the rotation.

"Joe stuck with me," Boddicker admits. "I pitched a shutout my first time out but struggled for a while after that. After 10 starts, I was only 4–4 with a 4.02 earned run average, so I've got to give him credit."

Boddicker blossomed after the slow start, winning 12 of 16 decisions in his last 17 innings to rank second among the Orioles in wins (16), complete games (10), and strikeouts (120). His 2.77 ERA ranked second in the American League.

PLAYOFF HERO

The best was yet to come for the 26-year-old freshman; named to pitch the second game of the American League Championship Series, he again produced a timely five-hit shutout against the slugging Chicago White Sox—this time with a career-high 14 strikeouts included. Boddicker, who had led all regular-season pitchers with five shutouts in AL play, won playoff MVP honors and entered the World Series with such confidence that he handcuffed the Philadelphia Phillies, 4–1, in Game 2 of an eventual five-game Baltimore victory.

Altobelli remembers the playoff game well. "We needed that game so badly," the manager recalls. "To see a rookie come into that situation and fan 14 has to make it maybe the best performance you've ever seen.

"As baseball men, we're all attuned to the strong-armed pitcher. Though he throws right-handed, Mike is a finesse pitcher in the style of a lot of lefthanders, people like Tommy John, Randy Jones, and Eddie Lopat. He uses his head and every game is an outstanding effort."

Though the Orioles sank to a fifth place finish and 19-game deficit last summer, Boddicker defied the sophomore jinx by becoming the league's lone 20-game winner, as well as its earned run

Mike Boddicker, a post-season star as a 1983 rookie, fanned a career-high 14 batters in a crucial Championship Series win over the Chicago White Sox. The lone 20-game winner in the American League last year has thrived under the guidance of patient Oriole Manager Joe Altobelli.

average champion (2.79). With four shutouts and 16 complete games, he missed ties for league leadership by one in each department.

"Nobody pitched better," said Texas lefthander Frank Tanana last fall. "It doesn't matter that his team didn't win. He deserves the Cy Young Award."

Boddicker did get three first-place votes but had to settle for a fourth-place finish behind relievers Willie Hernandez and Dan Quisenberry and fellow righthanded starter Bert Blyleven.

"To me," said Oriole pitching coach Ray Miller,

Baltimore pitching coach Ray Miller believes that Boddicker, not Willie Hernandez, should have won the 1984 Cy Young Award in the American League.

"the Cy Young Award means consistency, and nobody's been more consistent than Boddicker in 1984. With any kind of support, he would have had 20 wins long before the end of the season. He fields better than any other pitcher and he's as tough as they come. He worked one game with raw fingers and another when the trainer had to pound on his back between innings because his back spasms were so bad.

"He's an intelligent kid who can take what he has on any given day and win with it—just like (retired) Jim Palmer used to do. And he can tell you what he threw to a hitter the first time he faced him."

MIXED BAG

The 5-11, 172-pound native of Cedar Rapids, Iowa (he still lives in Norway, southwest of his hometown) keeps hitters off-stride with a diverse repertoire that includes a fastball, curve, slider, knuckleball, changeup, and a one-of-a-kind delivery he calls a foshball. Boddicker came up with the unusual name by noting that the pitch combined the action of a forkball with a changeup (known to the Orioles as a "dead fish").

"He gets great action on the ball," insists catcher Rick Dempsey. "He's got a great bunch of pitches, throws them all at different speeds, and can drop down and throw them sidearm, too. Even his fastball isn't bad (estimated speed is 86 miles per hour)."

The Minnesota Twins, a team of young sluggers who thrive on the fastball, learned that lesson on August 26, 1983, when Boddicker threw his second major-league shutout. The Oriole righthander, bothered by a blister on his pitching hand, couldn't throw his curve or changeup.

"All he had was a fastball against a fastball-hitting team," Ray Miller remembers. "He moved it in and out and shut them out."

BRIGHT KID

Pitching with the head instead of the arm is a Mike Boddicker trademark. "Velocity is over-rated," he insists. "The key is to keep hitters off balance by mixing speeds and changing locations. To get them to jump off-balance at what you're throwing instead of waiting on your pitches is the way to win games."

The one-time high school basketball star repeated his slow start of 1983 by losing his first three decisions last year. Then he won 18 of 24—with a 2.48 ERA—and had four starts left to reach the coveted 20-win circle. He did it on September 29 with a 12-hit triumph over the hard-hitting Boston Red Sox at Fenway Park.

Uncharacteristic wildness hurt Boddicker in the early stages of the '84 campaign. "I had to tell myself to throw strikes," he recalls. "I knew I could beat people—I had proven it the year before. For some reason, I just couldn't throw the ball over the plate—even when it was 3-and-0 and I knew the guy would be taking. Obviously, I managed to make the adjustments necessary. Good hitters are constantly adjusting. To be a good pitcher, you've got to be constantly adjusting, too."

Though he often finishes what he starts (26 completions in 58 starts over the last two years), the feeling lingers that Mike Boddicker would be even more devastating with better bullpen support; the left-right relief combine of Tippy Martinez and Sammy Stewart had 11 wins and 30 saves in 1984 but individually their numbers were not impressive.

Joe Altobelli counts on a rebound from them—and more of the same from Mike Boddicker, the ace Earl Weaver thought was a joker.

BOB BRENLY
BEACON IN THE FOG

YEAR	CLUB	AVG.	G	AB	R	H	2B	3B	HR	RBI	SB
		CAREER RECORD									
1976	Great Falls	.314	25	86	16	27	5	1	1	17	1
	Fresno	.367	17	60	16	22	3	1	1	9	1
1977	Cedar Rapids	.271	136	499	85	135	16	1	22	73	6
1978	Fresno	.284	135	489	102	139	34	5	17	89	12
1979	Fresno	.307	56	212	49	65	11	2	9	37	6
	Shreveport	.295	64	193	33	57	8	1	9	30	0
1980	Shreveport	.300	2	10	2	3	0	0	1	3	1
	Phoenix	.258	84	287	34	74	9	6	7	45	2
1981	Phoenix	.292	76	257	42	75	11	3	7	41	2
	San Francisco	.333	19	45	5	15	2	1	1	4	0
1982	San Francisco	.283	65	180	26	51	4	1	4	15	6
1983	San Francisco	.224	104	281	36	63	12	2	7	34	10
1984	San Francisco	.291	145	506	74	147	28	0	20	80	6

While the 1984 San Francisco Giants were at spring training in Phoenix, Bob Brenly pulled a Joan Rivers. He went up to manager Frank Robinson and said, "Can we talk?"

Robinson, since replaced as pilot by Danny Ozark and finally Jim Davenport, was willing to listen—and willing to give Brenly, a .224 hitter in 1983, another shot at the everyday catching job. He was happily surprised when he did.

"The thing about Frank," Brenly said later, "is that he doesn't want to have much to do with you until you earn his respect."

The 6-2, 210-pound righthanded hitter wasted no time in doing just that. He had such a hot first half—with a .316 average at the All-Star break—that he made the National League squad, along with teammate Chili Davis (both failed in pinch-hitting appearances).

Brenly, who turned 31 in February, went on to record a .291 average with 20 home runs and 80 runs batted in. He became the first San Francisco catcher to reach the 20-homer level since Dick Dietz hit 22 in 1970.

CONFIDENCE PAYS OFF

"The biggest change in Bob is confidence," suggested batterymate Mike Krukow late last summer. "In the past, he was too tentative. This year, his attitude has been, 'I can do it. I'm good.'"

Brenly made believers of the Atlanta Braves last year. He reached Pete Falcone for a grand slam at Candlestick Park on June 6, then exploded for his first four-hit game, in Atlanta on August 4. He capped the month of August with an

Bob Brenly, overlooked during most of 1983, became a surprise slugger for San Francisco last summer. He did not, however, surprise *himself* with his hitting prowess; as a collegian, he broke numerous Ohio University records established by Mike Schmidt.

inside-the-park home run at Montreal's Olympic Stadium and was named the team's Player-of-the-Month. Some dog days—Brenly's August stats included a .312 average, eight homers, and 29 RBI.

"He's a one-man wrecking crew," said Mets' manager Davey Johnson after a pair of Brenly homers gave the Giants a come-from-behind 7–6 win in the opener of a summer Friday twi-nighter. "He obliterated our staff. Three-run homers seem like a common occurrence with him."

Actually, Brenly's first home run came with only one man on base—off starter Ron Darling. It was the second blow—a three-run job off New York relief ace Jesse Orosco—that fueled Johnson's ire.

Though he never hit home runs in double figures once he reached the high minors, Brenly never regarded himself as a slouch either at the plate or behind it. In fact, his hitting made him a College All-American selection—when he broke or tied several Ohio University records held by Mike Schmidt. Brenly was a third baseman as a senior but had caught in his junior year. The combination of power and versatility seemed certain to attract considerable interest in the annual draft of amateur free agents—or so Brenly thought.

NO TAKERS

To his great surprise, no one so much as nibbled at the bait. The resounding silence hit him with the impact of a Mondale-sized defeat. Consoled by his wife Joan, a childhood friend from Coshocton, Ohio, Brenly continued to work out at the school's ballpark. Finally, the phone rang; the Giants needed an infielder for a rookie league team. No bonus, no up-front money, and not enough in the bank to pay for the trip. Brenly went, but he borrowed money to meet his expenses.

Five years later, at the Triple-A level, his career took a turn for the better. The Giants moved him off third base and back behind the plate. By 1981, he reached the majors and, on August 28, he homered off Pittsburgh reliever Rod Scurry in his first Candlestick Park at-bat.

He hit .333 in a 19-game trial that summer, but suffered a broken collarbone during the following spring training. Back in action on May 14, he singled with two out in the eighth to break up Steve Carlton's bid for his first no-hitter.

Though he went on to hit .283 that season, neither his power (four home runs) nor his erratic defense convinced Frank Robinson to make him the primary catcher. The search was on, but the team came up empty in trade talks. Those talks ended only after Brenly asserted himself last spring.

With his confidence growing daily, Brenly became San Francisco's most devastating power-hitter during his August hot streak. From August 20-26, he hit .440 (11-for-25) with four homers, seven runs scored, and 14 runs batted in, attracting enough attention to win the National League's Player-of-the-Week award.

He feasted on Montreal pitching, initiating a three-game series by collecting the game-winning RBI in the opener, a two-run homer in the second game, and the game-winning homer in the eleventh inning of the finale. At the end of that series, his batting average for the first seven games of the Giants' 12-game road trip stood at .464 (13-for-28).

"All I want to do is play," he said modestly at the time. "I feel comfortable playing every day. I'm tired and I'm sore, but I feel good about it."

GOOD GLOVEWORK

Ironically, Brenly won daily duty behind the plate because of his improved defense. He had only one RBI in April, but his throwing and handling of pitchers justified his presence in the lineup. The more he played, the more he hit—raising his average from .279 on April 28 to .357 at one point in the campaign. Another important average was his success ratio at erasing would-be base-stealers; he nailed 16 of the first 35 for a .457 percentage—not bad by big league standards.

"It's not physical ability," he said several times. "I've just busted my butt."

Considering that he played with a partial tear in the cartilage of his right knee after early June, it was even more amazing that Brenly was such a beacon in the San Francisco fog of 1984.

Postseason arthroscopic surgery—on both knees—repaired the damage and removed bone spurs. Though the right knee had also been operated on in 1983, Brenly is expected to enjoy a total recovery, according to Dr. Gordon Campbell, the Giants' orthopedic specialist.

That could be very bad news for National League pitchers.

GARY CARTER
FROM SHEA STADIUM TO COOPERSTOWN?

CAREER RECORD											
YEAR **CLUB**		**AVG.**	**G**	**AB**	**R**	**H**	**2B**	**3B**	**HR**	**RBI**	**SB**
1972	Cocoa	.239	18	71	6	17	3	0	2	9	1
	West Palm Beach	.320	20	50	9	16	2	2	0	5	0
1973	Quebec	.253	130	439	65	111	16	1	15	68	5
	Peninsula	.280	8	25	2	7	2	0	0	1	0
1974	Memphis	.268	135	441	62	118	14	7	23	83	6
	Montreal	.407	9	27	5	11	0	1	1	6	2
1975	Montreal	.270	144	503	58	136	20	1	17	68	5
1976	Montreal	.219	91	311	31	68	8	1	6	38	0
1977	Montreal	.284	154	522	86	148	29	2	31	84	5
1978	Montreal	.255	157	533	76	136	27	1	20	72	10
1979	Montreal	.283	141	505	74	143	26	5	22	75	3
1980	Montreal	.264	154	549	76	145	25	5	29	101	3
1981	Montreal	.251	100	374	48	94	20	2	16	68	1
1982	Montreal	.293	154	557	91	163	32	1	29	97	2
1983	Montreal	.270	145	541	63	146	37	3	17	79	1
1984	Montreal	.294	159	596	75	175	32	1	27	106	7

DIVISION SERIES RECORD											
YEAR **CLUB vs. OPP.**		**AVG.**	**G**	**AB**	**R**	**H**	**2B**	**3B**	**HR**	**RBI**	**SB**
1981	Montreal vs. Philadelphia	.421	5	19	3	8	3	0	2	6	0

LEAGUE CHAMPIONSHIP SERIES RECORD											
YEAR **CLUB vs. OPP.**		**AVG.**	**G**	**AB**	**R**	**H**	**2B**	**3B**	**HR**	**RBI**	**SB**
1981	Montreal vs. Los Angeles	.438	5	16	3	7	1	0	0	0	0

"Johnny Bench was probably the greatest catcher in the majors during the last 20 years," says Tommy Lasorda, manager of the Los Angeles Dodgers. "When he was having all his big years—all the homers, all the runs batted in—the Reds were having their greatest years.

"But a lot of their success depended on Bench's personality. He wasn't a rah-rah type of guy, but more a guy who you knew went out there and busted his butt every night. The other guys on the team knew he played hurt a lot, was playing a position where they almost never had anyone else to replace him, so they knew he *had* to be hurting a lot. Still, he went out there and did whatever he could, even though he obviously wasn't always at his best.

"You see a lot of the same thing in Gary Carter. He's a guy who plays hard, wants to win very badly. Plus, he obviously has a lot of ability. There's no reason he won't stay right on top of his position. He's certainly young enough."

HIGH PRAISE

Any comparison with Bench is high praise indeed for a catcher, but Lasorda isn't exaggerating. Carter—offensively and defensively—is clearly the premier receiver in the National League and probably in all of baseball—though fans of Lance Parrish, the rifle-armed backstop of the World Champion Detroit Tigers, would argue.

In 10 previous seasons, all with the Montreal Expos, the newly minted member of the New York Mets has played in seven All-Star games, including the last six in a row. Twice, in 1981 and 1984, he's been named Most Valuable Player of the midseason classic.

In the '81 game at Cleveland, Carter joined Ted Williams, Arky Vaughan, Al Rosen, and Willie McCovey as the only players to hit two home runs in an All-Star Game. Last year, his second-inning homer off Dave Stieb, the American League's starter, gave the Nationals a 2–1 lead that was never squandered (the final score was 3–1).

It's hardly surprising that Carter was the top vote-getter for the 1982 game, when he combined with Steve Rogers to form the first battery from the host city since Whitey Ford and Yogi Berra of the Yankees opened the 1960 game in New York.

All he did in 1984, when he was voted Montreal's Player-of-the-Year for the fourth time, was to establish career highs with 106 runs batted in (tied with Mike Schmidt for tops in the National League), a .294 batting average, 175 hits, and 16 game-winning RBI. He also hammered 27 home runs—the sixth time he's hit at least 20 in a season.

HAMPERED BY INJURY

Had it not been for a sore right knee—which required post-season arthroscopic surgery on October 5—Carter might have become the fourth catcher in baseball history to hit .300, slam 30 or more homers, and top 100 RBI in one season. The others—hardly shabby company—were Hall of Famers Gabby Hartnett and Roy Campanella, along with Walker Cooper.

At age 31, Carter seems to be on a Hall of Fame course too. The 6-2, 210-pound righthanded hitter has hit 215 lifetime home runs, 31 of them in a single season. He's clearly the best receiver in the 24-year history of the Mets—but the team

paid a high price to get him last December 10.

New York parted with slugging shortstop Hubie Brooks, second-year catcher Mike Fitzgerald, rookie centerfielder Herm Winningham, and top-rated pitching prospect Floyd Youmans, reputed to have the raw-but-undeveloped talent of Met mainstay Dwight Gooden, a former high school teammate.

From the perspective of New York general manager Frank Cashen, Carter was worth the sacrifice. "This is a banner day for the Mets," he said when the swap was announced. "We needed another righthanded power-hitter and they don't come much better than Gary Carter."

The player was also ecstatic. "As a 5-and-10

Carter's veteran guidance is expected to prove especially beneficial to the young pitching staff of the New York Mets.

Carter, whose 106 RBI tied Mike Schmidt for league leadership last year, has hit 215 lifetime home runs—unusual power production for a catcher.

man (five years with the same club and ten years in the majors), I could have vetoed the trade," he suggested. "I didn't because I was well aware of the nucleus of the Mets. I hope to be able to put them over the top and into the World Series. That is one of my most important career ambitions.

"Ambition has always been a great motivating force in my life," says Carter, who keeps a record of every game he plays and studies those records in the hope of finding paths to improvement. "If you put your mind to it, you can achieve what you want to achieve. I realized at a young age I had the ability to play baseball, so athletics were a part of my life very early."

"If I'm regarded as the best catcher in baseball, I want to go out there and do the best I can. I want to make the plays in the field. I hate to make an error. I want to catch every ball, throw everybody out, do everything I possibly can behind the plate. All in all, I just want to contribute to the team so we can get into the World Series."

Though regarded as perennial contenders, the closest the Expos came to a World Series berth was a ninth-inning, one-run loss to the Los Angeles Dodgers in the decisive fifth game of the 1981 National League Championship Series. The loss was no fault of Carter's; he hit .438 against the Dodgers, several points higher than the .421 he hit against the Philadelphia Phillies in the Eastern Divisional Series of that strike-torn split season.

BASEBALL OVER FOOTBALL

A three-sport star at Sunnyhills High School in Fullerton, California, Carter bypassed 100 college football scholarship offers to sign a $42,500 bonus contract with the Expos, who had drafted him in the third round of the amateur draft, on

June 23, 1972. Then he got the shock of his life: Montreal wanted Gary to become a catcher.

"It was very frustrating and discouraging," recalls Carter, who spent his schoolboy days as a pitcher, shortstop, and third baseman. "I was the worst catcher you ever saw—a real joke."

Even after two years of learning the tools of the trade in the minors and Puerto Rican Winter League, Carter was having so many problems that Double-A manager Karil Kuehl charged him a quarter for every ball he dropped (sometimes a dozen or more per game).

He reached the ragged Expos—still suffering from the growing pains of their 1969 birth as an expansion entry—billed as the team's "catcher of the future." But Gene Mauch stuck with incumbent Barry Foote behind the plate and placed Carter in the outfield.

At least the club had the benefit of Carter's booming bat; his .270 average and 17 homers earned him a second-place finish (to John Montefusco) in the NL Rookie-of-the-Year voting and a first-place finish in the balloting for Montreal's Player-of-the-Year.

A broken thumb, broken hand, and collision with an outfield fence slowed his progress the next season, but new manager Dick Williams restored the youngster's confidence and enthusiasm by making him a full-time catcher in 1977.

"I went head-to-head with Barry Foote in spring training," Carter recalls. "I had a phenomenal spring and he kind of curled up and died. He was traded to the Phillies in June."

The durable Carter has been a catcher since; he established career peaks in both at-bats and games played in 1984.

Carter has also established numerous career peaks in cooperation with the media and courtesy to his fans. The NL East's answer to Steve Garvey has never met an autograph hound he didn't like. His picture adorns thousands of den walls—the result of endless hours of posing with fans, especially during spring training.

A family man whose three children greet his return home with applause, Carter is close to his father and his brother and talks in loving terms of his mother, who died of leukemia when Carter was 12.

He hasn't been spoiled by a contract that will pay him $1.8 million per year through 1989; he makes a point of treating everyone he meets with sensitivity and civility. Only on the field is he aggressive and competitive.

"Like me, he thinks he's the best," says Cincinnati manager Pete Rose, a former teammate. "I don't think he has any weaknesses."

JOSE CRUZ
ANONYMOUS ACE OF THE ASTROS

	CAREER RECORD										
YEAR	CLUB	AVG.	G	AB	R	H	2B	3B	HR	RBI	SB
1967	St. Petersburg	.278	78	205	33	57	8	9	1	20	6
1968	Modesto	.286	133	504	101	144	24	10	13	53	17
1969	Arkansas	.273	102	400	56	109	18	9	6	49	4
1970	Arkansas	.300	133	493	89	148	29	7	21	90	11
	St. Louis	.353	6	17	2	6	1	0	0	1	0
1971	Tulsa	.327	67	254	56	83	15	7	15	49	5
	St. Louis	.274	83	292	46	80	13	2	9	27	6
1972	St. Louis	.235	117	332	33	78	14	4	2	23	9
1973	St. Louis	.227	132	406	51	92	22	5	10	57	10
1974	St. Louis	.261	107	161	24	42	4	3	5	20	4
1975	Houston	.257	120	315	44	81	15	2	9	49	6
1976	Houston	.303	133	439	49	133	21	5	4	61	28
1977	Houston	.299	157	579	87	173	31	10	17	87	44
1978	Houston	.315	153	565	79	178	34	9	10	83	37
1979	Houston	.289	157	558	73	161	33	7	9	72	36
1980	Houston	.302	160	612	79	185	29	7	11	91	36
1981	Houston	.267	107	409	53	109	16	5	13	55	5
1982	Houston	.275	155	570	62	157	27	2	9	68	21
1983	Houston	.318	160	594	85	189	28	8	14	92	30
1984	Houston	.312	160	600	96	187	28	13	12	95	22

	DIVISION SERIES RECORD										
YEAR	CLUB vs. OPP.	AVG.	G	AB	R	H	2B	3B	HR	RBI	SB
1981	Houston vs. Los Angeles	.300	5	20	0	6	1	0	0	0	1

	LEAGUE CHAMPIONSHIP SERIES RECORD										
YEAR	CLUB vs. OPP.	AVG.	G	AB	R	H	2B	3B	HR	RBI	SB
1980	Houston vs. Philadelphia	.400	5	15	3	6	1	1	0	4	0

The scouting report is out on Jose Cruz: give him a good mix of pitches and hope he swings—and misses—at the ones that are far off the plate.

"I can hit anything," says the 37-year-old left-fielder of the Houston Astros. "If I see the ball, I hit it. If I take a close pitch, the umpire calls it a strike and I don't like to fall behind on the count. So I go up there hacking."

Warned by Houston batting coach Denis Menke not to swing at too many bad pitches, the 6-0, 185-pound lefthanded hitter led his team in every offensive department except game-winning

Though he's not nationally known, quiet-but-steady Jose Cruz has won a record five Most Valuable Player citations from the media covering the Astros. A dangerous lefthanded hitter who hits line drives into the power alleys, Cruz should increase his home run total now that the Astrodome fences have been shortened.

runs batted in last year. His .312 batting average ranked fifth in the league, and he was also among the leaders with 96 runs scored, 95 runs batted in, 187 hits, 13 triples, and a .381 on-base percentage.

Yet his name remains virtually unknown outside of Houston. He didn't even make the National League All-Star squad in 1984.

"Not getting a lot of attention doesn't bother me," he insists. "I just want to do a job for the Astros."

ACQUIRED FROM CARDINALS

The veteran leftfielder has been doing that ever since Houston purchased his contract from St. Louis on October 24, 1974. With five .300 seasons—all for the Astros—since first coming to the majors in 1970, Jose Cruz has become the most popular player in Puerto Rico since the late Roberto Clemente. He's also riding a popularity wave in the Astrodome, where the public address announcer delights in stretching his name whenever he comes to bat: CRUUUUUZZZ!!!

Though fans around the country apparently

don't know enough to choose him as an All-Star starter, fellow National League players have saved him from the embarrassment of a reputation as the Rodney Dangerfield of baseball. At the conclusion of the 1984 campaign, they chose him, along with two-time Most Valuable Player Dale Murphy and batting champion Tony Gwynn, as the best outfielders in the circuit. According to Astros' manager Bob Lillis, the honor was well deserved.

"The thing about Cruz is he works hard, he's all business, and he has fun doing it," Lillis insists.

"He's a tough act to follow," chimes in Jerry Mumphrey, who follows Cruz in a Houston batting order known more for the line-drive, gap double than the home run.

It was Mumphrey, arriving from the New York Yankees, who made the All-Star squad last summer; Cruz, saddled with a .238 average on June 23, says he didn't deserve the honor. Maybe not on June 23, but—to the dismay of enemy pitchers—things quickly reverted to expected form.

Over the next five weeks, Cruz catapulted to the top of the batting derby with a 51-for-100 tear, a .510 batting average. He had 10 doubles, a triple, and three homers, knocking in 16 runs. He was Player of the Week for the period from June 25 to July 1 and Player of the Month for July.

POWER FOR THE ROAD

Though not known as a home run hitter—he failed to hit any of his 12 home runs at the Astrodome last season—Cruz managed to hit for power during his streak. On July 24, he homered twice in Candlestick Park, the windblown home of the San Francisco Giants.

"I'm back where I belong," he said near the end of the hitting tear. "I think I'm a .300 hitter. I've proven that in the past."

At age 37 (he turns 38 in August), Jose Cruz has his sights set on winning the batting title. If he realizes that goal, he'll become the oldest National League leader since 36-year-old Stan Musial won it in 1957. Not too many people are willing to bet against him.

"Throw the ball three feet over his head and outside, and he'll hit it down the left field line," complains Dodger pitcher Pat Zachry. "Three feet over his head inside, and he goes to right."

Cruz, whose brothers Heity and Tommy also played in the majors, is blessed with a natural swing that produces more than his share of line drives as well as infield choppers that scoot through the swift artificial grass of the Astrodome infield. Those that don't get through often become hits anyway; Cruz still runs well (his 22 steals led the 1984 Astros) despite his advanced baseball age.

The popular Houston outfielder began to hone his skills as a four-sport performer at Arroyo High School, where he picked up the nickname Cheo and made his father, a farmer and grocer, proud of his athletic prowess.

To maintain peak production, the Astro batting leader lifts light weights, does some stretching, and runs several miles at a time with Victor Lopez, who coaches the women's track team at Rice University. Cruz also keeps in shape by playing in the Puerto Rican Winter League.

All that activity seems to leave little time for wife Zoraida and the four Cruz children, but Jose manages to be an attentive father—and still finds time for swimming, hunting, deep-sea fishing, and tinkering with vintage automobiles.

CLOSER TARGET

The Astros will never tinker with the star, but they are tinkering with the outfield fences of the Astrodome, heretofore a graveyard for home run hitters. With shorter fences, Jose Cruz could become even more of a threat. He may be getting older, but he's also getting better.

Jose Cruz heads into the new season as the odds-on favorite to win his fifth Astros' MVP award; no one else has won it more than three times in the club's 22-year history. Cruz was a runaway winner in 1984—even though he confessed that he altered his swing for road games, going for home runs on the road but just singles and doubles in the vast reaches of the Astrodome. Closer fences at home will make such alterations unnecessary, according to Astro management.

"If the fences were moved in just 10 feet down the line and 15 feet in the alleys, you'd see a world of difference," insists Denis Menke, the hitting coach. "You'd see our hitters being far more aggressive, driving the ball more frequently. And this would carry over onto the road."

General Manager Al Rosen agrees. "I'm convinced players get mentally depressed hitting in the Dome over a long period of time. Consciously or unconsciously, they change their stroke in the Dome. And you just can't hit one way at home and another way on the road and be consistently successful."

That may be true for most players, but Jose Cruz is something special. Houston management knows that, but it also knows that making the Astrodome conform with other ball parks could have a significant influence on the statistics of its slugging leftfielder. And it salivates at the thought.

ALVIN DAVIS
ROOKIE ON THE RAMPAGE

		CAREER RECORD									
YEAR	CLUB	AVG.	G	AB	R	H	2B	3B	HR	RBI	SB
1982	Lynn	.284	74	225	37	64	10	1	12	56	1
1983	Chattanooga	.296	131	422	87	125	24	3	18	83	7
1984	Seattle	.284	152	267	80	161	34	3	27	116	5

Alvin Davis gave no hint of things to come when he was in the minor leagues. Selected by the Seattle Mariners in the sixth round of the June 1982 amateur free agent draft, the Arizona State University graduate first reported to Lynn, Massachusetts, in the Double-A Eastern League. In 74 games, he hit .284 with 12 home runs and 56 runs batted in.

That performance did not convince Mariner management to advance him to Triple-A ball, and Davis again found himself at the Double-A level in 1983, this time at Chattanooga of the Southern League.

The 6-1, 190-pound line-driver hitter was good enough to make the All-Star team, but his numbers were hardly electrifying: 296, 18 homers, 83 runs batted in.

With two other lefthanded-hitting first basemen ahead of him on the Seattle roster, all Davis could hope for last spring was an invitation to the big-league camp in Tempe, Arizona.

"I just wanted to show people what I could do, what my tools were, what I was capable of doing aginst major league pitching," recalls Davis, whose .400 spring with Seattle wasn't enough to preclude another minor-league exile. "I didn't expect to make the club."

QUICK RECALL

Sent to Salt Lake City, the club's Triple-A affiliate, Davis was playing his first game of the 1984 season when manager Bobby Floyd lifted him in the seventh inning. Wondering what he did wrong, the quiet, unassuming athlete soon got a pleasant surprise: Seattle wanted him back.

The Mariners hadn't planned it that way, but the unlucky break suffered by first baseman Ken Phelps—a broken finger on April 8—proved to be a lucky break for Alvin Davis.

"The best thing I did for this team was to get hurt," says Phelps, who hit 24 homers in 101 games.

In his second at-bat, Davis slugged a three-run homer to beat Dennis Eckersley, then with Boston. In his eighth plate appearance, his ninth-inning home run off Ron Davis tied a game with Minnesota. His third homer also came in the ninth—against Bill Caudill of Oakland on April 16. Three homers in his first five games made an immediate impression on Mariner management, not to mention Seattle fans, but Davis maintained a wary eye for what he thought would be in the inevitable ax. Only one thing could keep him in Seattle when Phelps returned, the rookie reasoned: a hot bat.

HIGH NUMBER

The man who wore Number 61—usually reserved for minor leaguers—to spring training let his bat do the talking for him; he hammered seven homers and knocked in 17 runs in his first 16 games, silencing skeptics who complained that Del Crandall, then Mariner manager, should have used veteran Pat Putnam instead of Davis when Phelps got hurt.

Davis finished May with 11 home runs and, by the July 10 All-Star Game, had a .287 average, 18 homers, and 65 RBI. Though he plays the position of Rod Carew, Eddie Murray, Don Mattingly, Kent Hrbek, Cecil Cooper, and Andre Thornton, Davis made the American League squad as Seattle's lone representative.

He batted once—as a pinch-hitter for pitcher Jack Morris—and struck out against Dwight Gooden of the New York Mets. It was the only head-to-head confrontation of the two rising stars who would win Rookie-of-the-Year honors for 1984.

Teammate Mark Langston, who won a club-record 17 games and led the American League in strikeouts, was the only serious challenger Davis had in the AL rookie race. By year's end, few could argue with the achievements of the powerful first baseman, who drove in the most runs by a rookie since Walt Dropo of the 1950 Red Sox had 144 and Al Rosen had 116. Fred Lynn and Jim Rice (1975) and Ron Kittle (1983) are the only American League freshmen to notch 100 RBI in a season since.

"You see a lot of young talent," says 14-year veteran Don Baylor, the powerful designated hitter of the New York Yankees. "But when you see Alvin Davis, you're really seeing something. And you're going to *really* be seeing something."

About the only baseball insider who wasn't surprised by the slugger's sensational debut was Seattle batting coach Ben Hines.

"Davis knows a good pitch almost before it's pitched," explains Hines, who was the hitting instructor at Arizona State when Davis compiled successive batting averages of .279, .370, .395, and

Alvin Davis made the most of a lucky break—a fractured finger suffered by seattle first baseman Ken Phelps put him in a starting role.

.351 for the Sun Devils. "He makes a judgment on the ball early and knows at the release point what kind of ball it's going to be and where it's going to go. You'd like to give that to everybody just like you give them a mother and father. It makes a young player look like an experienced player."

VETERAN'S ANALYSIS

Gorman Thomas, a one-time American League home run king who was injured much of last year, also sees uncanny poise in Alvin Davis.

"He walks around like a 10-year veteran," Thomas says. "He doesn't promote himself. A lot of guys in his position would be walking around asking if you want their autograph. He just goes about things in a professional way. He doesn't dress flamboyantly and he always has a smile for you."

Talent is another key factor in the rise of Alvin Davis, according to Thomas. "He has a very fluid, short, compact, and very powerful swing," says the former Milwaukee outfield star. "He's aggressive to the point where he knows what pitches to be aggressive on. He's also a patient hitter and that's remarkable for a rookie. I haven't seen him look bad in one time at bat."

Seattle general manager Hal Keller, who headed the scouting department of the Mariners when Davis was drafted, is even more lavish in his praise. "As a young hitter, he's the best judge of the strike zone since Ted Williams," Keller insists.

Pitchers never questioned that knowledge, but they did question the ability of the rookie to hit major league curveballs. In July, after Davis had fattened his batting average by feasting on fastballs, the endless diet of slow stuff and breaking balls began. He hit .235 with three homers for the month.

"I was beginning to learn myself," Davis says in retrospect. "I knew I had to go through it, that everything would be a learning experience to build upon.

"The main thing I learned is that I still have a lot to learn. I'm pleased with the season I had, but I have a lot of improving to do."

That's quite a statement coming from a hitter who bats third in his team's lineup, hit two grand slams and seven three-run homers as a rookie, and was such a consistent hitter that his average stood at .287 for the first half and .281 for the second. He also was intentionally passed 16 times, more than any rookie in baseball history.

"He and Don Mattingly are two of the best young hitters I've seen in years," says Sparky Anderson, manager of the World Champion Detroit Tigers. Being mentioned in the same breath with Mattingly is not too shabby; all the Yankee star did last year was hit .343, tops in the league.

CONVERTED FROM THIRD

A high school third baseman in Riverside, California, Davis seems to have an unlimited future at age 24 (he'll be 25 shortly after Labor Day). He may also have a future as a colorful character; at the same time a real estate agent was trying to peddle Davis a $200,000 house after his hot start, the first baseman asked a team official if it was safe to lease an apartment. He once kept roommate Phil Bradley awake by patiently talking to every New York writer who phoned. He also answered every piece of fan mail—a job that became more burdensome as the season wore on—and even supplied the stamps himself.

Alvin Davis has, in one short season, put his own stamp on the American League. Rival pitchers would just as soon mark him RETURN TO SENDER.

STEVE GARVEY
A VETERAN WITH CLASS

CAREER RECORD

YEAR	CLUB	AVG.	G	AB	R	H	2B	3B	HR	RBI	SB
1968	Ogden, Pioneer	.338	62	216	49	73	12	3	20*	59*	9
1969	Albuquerque	.373	83	316	51	118	18	2	14	85	9
1969	Los Angeles	.333	3	3	0	1	0	0	0	0	0
1970	Spokane, PCL	.319	95	376	71	120	26	5	15	87	13
1971	Los Angeles	.227	81	225	27	51	12	1	7	26	1
1972	Los Angeles	.269	96	294	36	79	14	2	9	30	4
1973	Los Angeles	.304	114	349	37	106	17	3	8	50	0
1974	Los Angeles	.312	156	642	95	200	32	3	21	111	5
1975	Los Angeles	.319	160	659	85	210	38	6	18	95	11
1976	Los Angeles	.317	162x	631	85	200	37	4	13	80	19
1977	Los Angeles	.297	162x	646	91	192	25	3	33	115	9
1978	Los Angeles	.316	162x	639	89	202*	36	9	21	113	10
1979	Los Angeles	.315	162	648	92	204	32	1	28	110	3
1980	Los Angeles	.304	163*	658	78	200*	27	1	26	106	6
1981	Los Angeles	.283	110x	431	63	122	23	1	10	64	3
1982	Los Angeles	.282	162x	625	66	176	35	1	16	86	5
1983	San Deigo	.294	100	388	76	114	22	0	14	59	4
1984	San Diego	.284	161	617	72	175	27	2	8	86	1

*—Led league   x—Tied for league lead

DIVISION SERIES RECORD

YEAR	CLUB vs. OPP.	AVG.	G	AB	R	H	2B	3B	HR	RBI	SB
1981	Los Angeles vs. Houston	.368	5	19	4	7	0	1	2	4	0

LEAGUE CHAMPIONSHIP SERIES RECORD

YEAR	CLUB vs. OPP.	AVG.	G	AB	R	H	2B	3B	HR	RBI	SB
1974	Los Angeles vs. Pittsburgh	.389	4	18	4	7	1	0	2	5	0
1977	Los Angeles vs. Philadelphia	.308	4	13	2	4	0	0	0	0	1
1978	Los Angeles vs. Philadelphia	.389	4	18	6	7	1	1	4	7	0
1981	Los Angeles vs. Montreal	.286	5	21	2	6	0	0	1	2	0
1984	San Diego vs. Chicago	.400	5	20	1	8	1	0	1	7	0

WORLD SERIES RECORD

YEAR	CLUB vs. OPP.	AVG.	G	AB	R	H	2B	3B	HR	RBI	SB
1974	Los Angeles vs. Oakland	.381	5	21	2	8	0	0	0	1	0
1977	Los Angeles vs. New York	.375	6	24	5	9	1	1	1	3	0
1978	Los Angeles vs. New York	.208	6	24	1	5	1	0	0	0	1
1981	Los Angeles vs. New York	.417	6	24	3	10	1	0	0	0	0
1984	San Diego vs. Detroit	.200	5	20	2	4	2	0	0	2	0

Fans of the San Diego Padres won't forget the date: December 21, 1982. That is the day Steve Garvey ended a 12-year career with the Los Angeles Dodgers to sign a five-year, $6.6 million contract with the Padres. It was also the day that San Diego became a team to reckon with in the National League West.

With Garvey on board and some of the prized prospects from the farm system ready to blossom, the Padres took tremendous bargaining power into the free agent market one year after garnering Garvey's autograph. For the second straight off-season, San Diego's powers of persuasion paid handsome dividends; Rich (Goose) Gossage, sensing his talents could put the Padres over the top, inked a five-year package estimated to be worth $6.25 million.

The acquisition of Graig Nettles, like Gossage a key Yankee suffering from disenchantment in New York, and the conversion of outfielder Alan Wiggins to second base, were the missing links to the puzzle as San Diego won its first pennant.

Not surprisingly, Steve Garvey, a veteran with four years of World Series experience, was the key.

He led the Padres with 86 runs batted in—15 of them game winners—and hit .284 with 27 doubles and eight home runs in 161 games. He was even better in the field, where he played such flawless defense that he broke Mike Hegan's record of 178 consecutive errorless games at first base. The Padre pillar was perfect in the field—no errors in 160 games—and takes a record streak of 189 into the 1985 season.

OCTOBER HERO

Last year, Garvey's regular-season contributions went almost unnoticed outside of San Diego, because the Padres won the Western Division with a 12-game bulge. The National League Championship Series was a different story, how-

ever. There, with the Padres facing a 2–0 deficit in the best-of-five playoff, Garvey turned Lone Ranger, riding to the rescue in the nick of time.

After Kevin McReynolds and Garry Templeton combined for five RBI to produce a 7–1 victory in game three, Garvey stole the fourth game with a display of clutch hitting that left the Cubs shaking their heads in disbelief. He had four hits in five at-bats, including a double and a one-out, two-run homer that won the game in the bottom of the ninth. He knocked in a total of five runs, contributed another the next day, and finished the playoffs with a .400 average (8-for-20), seven RBI, and his third MVP award in five Championship Series appearances.

He's been MVP in the All-Star Game twice and, in the 1984 game, scored the first run in the National League's 3–1 victory. It was the ninth time the fans have voted him a starting berth on the team—and one of those victories was by write-in when his name was left off the ballot.

Garvey has also been National League MVP, with the 1974 Dodgers, and runner-up in the MVP voting, in 1978. The only honor that has eluded him is the World Series MVP award; he hit .417 in the 1981 Series—the only time he played on a winning team—but teammates Ron Cey, Steve Yeager, and Pedro Guerrero shared MVP honors.

KEY CONTRIBUTOR

"I wanted to help make the Padres a winner," he said. "I wanted to help build a winning baseball tradition. I think I've helped do that. I hope some of the younger guys here experience the same kind of day I had when I had the four hits against the Cubs. It doesn't last long, but as the years pass, it gets better all the time."

The soft-spoken, compact first baseman—some observers dispute his listed 5-10, 190-pound proportions in the San Diego media guide—is well known nationally not only because of his achievements on the field but also because he gives generously of his time to both media and fans. Jealous rivals, among other skeptics, charge he is deliberately cultivating a clean image as a potential springboard to politics after his playing career ends.

One of the true gentlemen of the game, Garvey became an October hero in his second San Diego season; ninth-inning homer in Game 4 of the Championship Series paved the way to the first Padre pennant. Excelling on defense as well as offense, he did not commit a single error in 160 games last season.

Californians Steve Garvey, first baseman of the San Diego Padres, and Reggie Jackson, designated hitter of the California Angels, meet during off-season athletic competition.

Garvey, who will turn 37 in December, doesn't deny an interest in running for United States Senator from California some day, but insists his first priorities are baseball and children Chrisha and Whitney. Steve and Cyndy Garvey, mother of the girls, seemed to have a storybook marriage—until that image was shattered when the ship of matrimony hit the rocks and Cyndy relocated cross-country to New York.

The former Michigan State All-American and later Number 1 draft choice of the Dodgers doesn't discourage his good guy image. He's patient with autograph seekers, tolerant of pushy media types, and has been known to thank those few writers who prepare intelligent questions in advance.

After one spring training interview during his Dodger days, Garvey turned to his inquisitor and said, "Thank you."

Stunned, the reporter replied, "Why are you thanking me? I should be thanking you."

"You did your homework," Garvey responded.

Asked whether any other player had ever thanked him for an interview, the reporter didn't hesitate. "No," he said. "Garvey was the first."

BOOMING BAT

On the field, Garvey lets his bat do the talking.

He's topped 100 RBI five times and 20 homers five times, with a career peak of 33 in 1977, the year he joined Dusty Baker, Ron Cey, and Reggie Smith as the only quartet of teammates to hit at least 30 homers each in the same season.

A lifetime .300 hitter going into the 1984 season, Garvey knows a good year will restore his average to the magic circle. Hitting third should help.

"I've always hit well batting third," he says. "I like hitting third because I'm a line-drive hitter and I like to play hit-and-run. You should be able to handle the bat if you're going to hit third."

The righthanded-hitting first baseman opened last season batting cleanup but moved to third in June after manager Dick Williams decided that Garvey was pressing—overswinging and hacking at bad pitches—from the fourth spot.

The switch worked, as Garvey unleashed a .432 streak over a 10-game span immediately after the move.

"There are two things that make Garvey a better hitter," Williams points out. "One is to purposely walk a batter to get to him. The other is to throw a pitch close to him."

No pitcher in his right mind would want to make Steve Garvey a better hitter. Unless that pitcher is wearing a San Diego uniform, of course.

KIRK GIBSON
POTENTIAL PAYS OFF

		CAREER RECORD										
YEAR	CLUB	AVG.	G	AB	R	H	2B	3B	HR	RBI	GW	SB
1978	Lakeland	.240	54	175	27	42	5	4	7	40		13
1979	Evansville	.245	89	327	50	80	13	5	9	42		20
	Detroit	.237	12	38	3	9	3	0	1	4	0	3
1980	Detroit	.263	51	175	23	46	2	1	9	16	1	4
1981	Detroit	.328	83	290	41	95	11	3	9	40	5	17
1982	Detroit	.278	69	266	34	74	16	2	8	35	6	9
1983	Detroit	.227	128	401	60	91	12	9	15	51	6	14
1984	Detroit	.282	149	531	92	150	23	10	27	91		29

	LEAGUE CHAMPIONSHIP SERIES RECORD										
YEAR	CLUB vs. OPP.	G	AB	R	H	RBI	2B	3B	HR	SB	BA
1984	Detroit vs. Kansas City	3	12	2	5	2	1	0	1	1	.417

	WORLD SERIES RECORD										
YEAR	CLUB vs. OPP.	G	AB	R	H	RBI	2B	3B	HR	SB	BA
1984	Detroit vs. San Diego	5	18	4	6	7	0	0	2	3	.333

Kirk Gibson would just as soon forget his first four seasons in the major leagues. He'd be more than happy to slip 1984 into a Xerox and make enough copies to last for a career.

The powerful rightfielder of the Detroit Tigers, capitalizing on his first clear shot at daily duty, not only began to cash in on advance billings that pictured him as the next Mickey Mantle but proved especially productive under the glare of the postseason spotlight.

The playoff MVP with a .417 average that included a home run, double, and stolen base, he also hit .333 with seven runs batted in during the five-game World Series against San Diego. Both his home runs came in the last game—a two-run shot in the first off Mark Thurmond and a titanic three-run blast off ace reliever Goose Gossage in the eighth.

"I've always wanted to be the guy to come through when the chips are down," says Gibson, who accepted a $200,000 bonus to bypass football offers and sign with the Tigers in 1978. "The chips were down because nobody wanted to go back to San Diego."

The Tigers—on the strength of Gibson's bat and the relief work of Willie Hernandez—wrapped up the World Series by sweeping the three games in Detroit following a split of the first two games in San Diego.

SWEET REVENGE

Gibson was especially grateful to apply the clincher against Gossage; the Goose, then with the New York Yankees, had fanned Gibson on three pitches when the hard-hitting lefthanded batter made his big-league debut in 1979.

Detroit manager Sparky Anderson had expected Gossage to walk Gibson in that situation—first base open and two out in the eighth with the righthand-hitting Lance Parrish due next—but Parrish had homered in the previous inning.

"Sparky held up four fingers to indicate they were going to put me on," Gibson remembers, "but I held up 10 to say, 'I bet you $10 I'm going to hit it out if he pitches to me.' All the great hitters in baseball seem to have a great intensity, great concentration when it counts. And that's what I was feeling."

A native of Pontiac, Michigan, whose boyhood heroes were Tiger stars Al Kaline and Bill Freehan, Gibson became a regular only after extensive tutoring sessions on outfield play with the man he succeeded in right field. "I'd always had a terrible time in right field," admits the former Michigan State flanker. "Kaline taught me how to play it. He had me charging ground balls and throwing after one step instead of two or three."

Kaline, a Hall of Famer who now telecasts Tiger games, was joined in coaching instruction by Gates Brown, a one-time star pinch-hitter who served as Detroit batting coach a year ago.

"He was his own worst enemy," says Brown of Gibson. "With all his strength, all he has to do is make contact and the home runs will come. A home run is a home run whether it goes 350 feet or 550 feet, but Gibson was trying to hit every ball over the roof."

TAPE-MEASURE SHOT

He did it once—connecting for a 600-foot blast into a lumber yard outside the stadium on June 14, 1983. Mickey Mantle, Harmon Killebrew, Frank Howard, and eight other strongmen had previously hit balls over the roof, but even that prodigious shot was not enough to win Gibson a regular spot in the lineup. Too many strikeouts, an anemic batting average, and erratic defense kept him sidelined. So did a series of injuries—to knee, wrist, collarbone, calf, and finger, among

other parts of the anatomy. Then there was the pressure of the press, who billed Gibson as the second coming of Al Kaline—when they weren't measuring him for the shoes of Mickey Mantle.

"What happened to me, I wouldn't wish on anyone," he says. "But I never broke. I got through it and it was a lesson in life, in growing up. I just had to do it in public. It was hard to understand I was a public figure. This is a humbling game and I hate to accept failure."

At one point, Gibson was so desperate to correct his flawed image that he hired a Hollywood PR firm to send out complementary photographs and arrange dates with starlets. But that compounded the problem, creating an inevitable comparison with the Joe DiMaggio–Marilyn Monroe tandem.

Getting into good shape would maximize Gibson's talents and minimize his proclivity to injury, the outfielder reasoned. By the time the Tigers assembled at Lakeland, Florida, for 1984 spring training, the muscular rightfielder was ready—and Sparky Anderson was delighted at both his physical and emotional condition.

After improving his defensive play considerably, Gibson found himself able to concentrate more at the plate. He became a more selective hitter, willing to go with the pitch and hit to the opposite field if necessary. On May 2, he hit a single, double, and triple to left—the opposite field—and a single to center.

MANY TALENTS

His game now complete, he not only hits with power but also bunts well and is a constant threat to steal (his 29 stolen bases were 10 more than the next-best Tiger in that department, Alan Trammell). One of two Tigers to top 90 runs batted in, Gibson finished the regular season with a .282 batting average, 10 triples, 27 homers, and 91 RBI—17 of them game winners. Only Eddie Murray of the Orioles had more game-winning RBI and only Harold Baines of the White Sox and Jim Rice of the Red Sox had as many as Gibson.

He was sixth in voting for Most Valuable Player in the American League, with only first-place finisher Willie Hernandez ranking ahead of him among the World Champion Tigers. Gibson's good showing in the writers' balloting was not surprising after a season in which only two American Leaguers—Gibson and Toronto's Lloyd Moseby—reached double figures in doubles, triples, homers, and stolen bases, with 90-plus RBI to boot. With three more homers and one more

Kirk Gibson finished a fine 1984 season by pounding a pair of homers against the Padres in the decisive fifth game of the World Series. Gibson says that coaching by Hall of Famer Al Kaline, once the Tiger rightfielder, helped him earn a regular job for the first time in 1984.

stolen base, Gibson would have joined Dale Murphy of the Atlanta Braves as the only active players who have stolen at least 30 bases and hit at least that many home runs in a single season. With continued improvement, Gibson could also become a strong candidate to join Hank Aaron as the only players in baseball history to reach 40 homers and 30 steals in the same season (no, Willie Mays never did it).

The Tigers should count their lucky stars they even have Kirk Gibson. As a youngster in Waterford, Michigan, his first love was football. A high school standout, he still holds Michigan State University records with 112 catches, 2,347 yards, and 24 touchdown receptions—statistics that convinced the St. Louis Cardinals of the National Football League to make him a seventh-round draft pick in 1979. But he had already been drafted by the Tigers—in the first round—after hitting .390 with 16 homers, 52 RBI, and 21 stolen bases in his lone season of college baseball.

Skeptics suggested he would become "the best wide receiver in the major leagues," but Gibson made them choke on those words. It just took a little time.

Sparky Anderson, who arrived in Tigertown in 1979, exercised enormous patience, sympathizing with Gibson as he staggered through a .227 campaign in 1983, the first year the outfielder played in more than 100 games. The raw ability was always there; it just had to be cooked to perfection. In 1984, it was—with just the right amount of seasoning thrown in.

DWIGHT GOODEN
WHAT NEXT FOR THE ROOKIE RAVE?

CAREER RECORD											
YEAR	CLUB	W-L	ERA	G	CG	ShO	SV	IP	H	BB	SO
1982	Kingsport (A)	5-4	2.47	9	4	2	0	66.	53	25	66
1982	Little Falls (A)	0-1	4.15	2	0	0	0	13.	11	3	18
1983	Lynchburg (A)	19-4	2.50	27	10	6	0	191.	121	112	300
1984	New York, NL	17-9	2.60	31	7	3	0	218	161	73	276

Before last season, no teenaged pitcher had stood the world on its ear since 17-year-old Bob Feller blazed his way through the American League with the 1936 Cleveland Indians.

Fresh off the farm (not the farm system) in Van Meter, Iowa, Feller cut a swath through AL hitters with the ease of a steak knife cutting through butter. He won five of eight decisions and fanned 76 batters in 62 innings. It wasn't until 1939, however, that Feller mushroomed into the star righthander whose fastball would prove the ticket to Cooperstown.

In 1984, Dwight Gooden accomplished in one season what took Feller four. After spending all of the previous season at the Class A level—save for three Triple-A starts in postseason play—Gooden pitched his way into the starting rotation of the New York Mets at age 19. With nothing to lose after the team had finished last in the six-team National League East the year before, rookie manager Davey Johnson pleaded with general manager Frank Cashen for the chance to keep Gooden on the big league roster. But even

Johnson was amazed at the results of that decision:

AMAZING SEASON

- Gooden's 276 strikeouts led the major leagues and broke the previous big league record for strikeouts by a rookie (Cleveland's Herb Score had 245 in 1955)
- His average of 11.39 strikeouts per nine innings smashed the old mark of 10.71 held by Sam McDowell of the 1965 Indians
- He twice fanned 16 in a game, the major league high (Mike Witt of California did it once) and had an NL record 43 whiffs over a three-game span in late summer
- The youngest player ever selected for the All-Star Game, he struck out the side—Lance Parrish, Chet Lemon, and Alvin Davis—in the first of the two scoreless innings he worked
- Apparently getting stronger and more confident as the season wore on, he pitched a one-hitter against the Cubs on September 7.

Dwight Gooden's 17-win, 276-strikeout season made him a runaway winner of NL Rookie-of-the-Year honors. His strong right arm enabled him to record back-to-back 16-strikeout games.

No wonder the Mets averaged 28,659 in home games Gooden worked but only 24,393 in all other games at Shea Stadium.

"I'm glad as hell every pitcher who comes into the game isn't like him," says Mike Schmidt, who tied for league leadership in home runs and runs batted in last season. "If that were the case, I'd change professions. It's not worth it."

After he lost a 2–1 game to Schmidt's Phillies on an eighth-inning balk in early September, Gooden drew lavish praise from the home run king.

"We hadn't faced him since June and the difference was incredible," Schmidt told reporters. "He was more confident and had a free and easy motion, which he didn't have last time. He didn't overthrow and his curve was a lot better. That's

tremendous improvement for a kid that age in less than three months. When Nolan Ryan or Gooden pitch, it's a special game—and I welcome the challenge of hitting against them."

The 6-3, 200-pound flamethrower, a nonsmoking, non-drinking introvert whose sense of humor suggests he may someday become a clubhouse prankster, also attracted the attention of Jim Frey, the one-time Mets batting coach who coaxed the Chicago Cubs to the championship of the National League East last year.

"He's the best young pitcher I ever saw," Frey says. "Better than Bob Gibson, Jim Palmer, or Nolan Ryan. He did things at 19 that Tom Seaver did at 23. When he's done in 15 years or so, we'll say, 'He was the best of his time.'"

AWARD POTENTIAL

Gooden, whose 17–9 record and 2.60 earned run average prompted a second-place finish in voting for the National League's Cy Young Award, came within a whisker of repeating the unprecedented parlay that Fernando Valenzuela managed in 1981: capturing Rookie-of-the-Year and Cy Young honors in the same season. But better things seem to lie ahead.

Gooden spent part of the off-season in the Florida Instructional League in an effort to improve his primary weakness: holding runners on base. In 1984, 47 of the 50 base runners who attempted to steal on him were successful.

Tutor John Cumberland, a former major-league pitcher who worked with Gooden at Lynchburg of the Carolina League in 1983, also taught him a changeup in Florida.

"I don't see how he can get much better mechanically," Cumberland says. "He's already in the category of Bob Gibson and Nolan Ryan—and he's only 20 years old. I taught him a change-up off his fastball motion and he's throwing it for strikes."

That's hardly good news for National League batters—or for the fans of teams who hope to stop the Mets from wresting the divisional title away from the Chicago Cubs.

With the changeup added to Gooden's basic fastball-curveball repertoire, hitters figure to be even more off-balance when they face him. And the few who reach base won't be able to run at will anymore.

Where does that leave the 1984 analysis of Philadelphia superscout Hugh Alexander, who called Gooden "the best young pitcher I've seen in 30 years—ahead of Bob Gibson at the same age"?

According to four-time batting champion Bill Madlock of the Pittsburgh Pirates, "Gooden could win four or five Cy Young Awards. He's the most powerful pitcher to come up in 10 years."

Only one player has won the Cy Young Award, established in 1956, as many as four times, and Steve Carlton, at 40 showing the effects of advancing baseball age, has probably seen his best days.

Not so for Gooden, who throws a rising fastball Pete Rose says compares favorably with the favorite pitch of Hall of Famer Sandy Koufax. Rose should know; he's the only hitter to face both.

"There's not much you can do when a guy throws a 2-2 pitch 95 miles an hour on the outside corner," says Detroit's Chet Lemon, one of Gooden's All-Star Game victims. "He's in a class by himself."

The youngest of six children, Gooden grew up in Tampa, became an Al Kaline fan after watching the long-time Tiger star hammer two home runs in a spring training game at Lakeland, and was playing outfield and third base in Little League by the time he was 10.

RELUCTANT PITCHER

A reluctant Little League pitcher at age 12, Gooden had earned a city-wide reputation within two years and began to think about a big-league future. After graduating from Hillsborough High School, Gooden was a first-round draft selection of the Mets in June 1982. But four teams picked other players ahead of him: Shawon Dunston (Cubs), Augie Schmidt (Blue Jays), Jimmy Jones (Padres), and Brian Oelkers (Twins).

"When I was a kid, Nolan Ryan and J. R. Richard were my favorite pitchers," reveals the Mets' instant star. "My friends always compared me with them in the Little Leagues. I didn't keep their clippings but I watched them on TV whenever they pitched.

"That doesn't mean I got caught up with striking guys out; my job is *getting* guys out. I'll take every first-pitch grounder to the shortstop I can get—it's easier on your arm anyway."

With the arm Dwight Gooden has, he shouldn't worry.

GOOSE GOSSAGE
THROWING THE GOLDEN EGG

CAREER RECORD

YEAR	CLUB	W-L	ERA	G	CG	ShO	SV	IP	H	BB	SO
1970	Sarasota, Gulf Coast	0-0	2.81	3	0	0	0	16	11	4	21
1970	Appleton, Midwest	0-3	5.91	10	0	0	0	35	41	19	21
1971	Appleton, Midwest	18-2	1.83	25	15	7	0	187	141	50	149
1972	Chicago, AL	7-1	4.28	36	0	0	2	80	72	44	57
1973	Chicago, AL	0-4	7.38	20	1	0	0	50	57	37	33
1973	Iowa, American Association	5-4	3.68	12	5	1	1	71	59	28	66
1974	Appleton, Midwest	0-2	3.38	2	0	0	0	8	8	4	5
1974	Chicago, AL	4-6	4.15	39	0	0	1	89	92	47	64
1975	Chicago, AL	9-8	1.84	62	0	0	26	142	99	70	130
1976	Chicago, AL	9-17	3.94	31	15	0	1	224	214	90	135
1977	Pittsburgh	11-9	1.62	72	0	0	26	133	78	49	151
1978	New York, AL	10-11	2.01	63	0	0	27	134	87	59	122
1979	New York, AL	5-3	2.64	36	0	0	18	58	48	19	41
1980	New York, AL	6-2	2.27	64	0	0	33x	99	74	37	103
1981	New York, AL	3-2	0.77	32	0	0	20	47	22	14	48
1982	New York, AL	4-5	2.23	56	0	0	30	93	63	28	102
1983	New York, AL	13-5	2.27	57	0	0	22	87½	82	25	90
1984	San Diego	10-6	2.90	62	0	0	25	102.1	75	36	84

x—Tied for league lead

DIVISION SERIES RECORD

YEAR	CLUB vs. OPP.	W-L	ERA	G	CG	ShO	SV	IP	H	BB	SO
1981	New York vs. Milwaukee	0-0	0.00	3	0	0	2	6⅔	3	2	8

LEAGUE CHAMPIONSHIP SERIES RECORD

YEAR	CLUB vs. OPP.	W-L	ERA	G	CG	ShO	SV	IP	H	BB	SO
1978	New York vs. Kansas City	1-0	4.50	2	0	0	1	4	3	0	3
1980	New York vs. Kansas City	0-1	54.00	1	0	0	0	⅓	3	0	0
1981	New York vs. Oakland	0-0	0.00	2	0	0	2	2⅔	1	0	2
1984	San Diego vs. Chicago	0-0	4.50	3	0	0	1	4	5	1	5

WORLD SERIES RECORD

YEAR	CLUB vs. OPP.	W-L	ERA	G	CG	ShO	SV	IP	H	BB	SO
1978	New York vs. Los Angeles	1-0	0.00	3	0	0	0	6	1	1	4
1981	New York vs. Los Angeles	0-0	0.00	3	0	0	2	5	2	2	5
1984	San Diego vs. Detroit	0-0	13.50	2	0	0	0	2.2	3	1	2

When Sir Edmund Hilary led a British team up the slopes of Mount Everest and returned in triumph, he was asked why he attempted the dangerous mission.

"Because it is there," he said.

Goose Gossage was the Mount Everest of San Diego last summer. Whenever a member of the Padres was asked where the team's new-found confidence had come from, the pat answer was, "Because he is there."

Team president Ballard Smith, who dredged the club's coffers for some $6.25 million to lure the Goose away from the American League, insists he would do it again.

"Absolutely, it's worth what he costs," the executive noted last summer. "Last year at this time, we were out of the pennant race. We're nine-and-a-half ahead now. Rich wasn't here last year; he is this year. Rich hasn't just saved games for us; he's also taken the pressure off our young pitching staff. They all know he's sitting out there in the bullpen."

The 6-3, 217-pound righthander, who turns 34 in July, had a direct hand in 35 of the 92 San Diego victories last season. He saved 25, won 10 others, and allowed an average of 2.9 earned runs per nine innings. He also fanned 84 in $102\frac{1}{3}$ innings, quieting skeptics who had suggested his once-feared fastball was fading.

"He's the key to our pen," manager Dick Williams told reporters. "He's really let us set it up, with the middle men and the short men. He's made our pen, which was a weakness, into a strength."

The Chicago Cubs will vouch for that; after the Padres scored four runs in the home seventh to take a 6–3 lead in the deciding playoff game, Gossage came out of the bullpen to slam the door for the final two innings. He struck out two, walked none, and yielded just two hits.

He wasn't nearly as effective in the World Series, with two appearances against Detroit, but his yeoman season helped make San Diego's first World Series possible.

"I'm glad we have him," Dick Williams says. "He's a crafty pitcher. His fastball may be his out pitch, but he does a lot more than throw the ball past batters."

FILLED THE VOID

Teammate Kurt Bevacqua, one of few Padre World Series stars, agrees: "We had a big hole in our bullpen and finished 10 games out of first place, so all the Goose had to do was make the difference in 11 games. He's obviously done that."

Goose Gossage, in his first San Diego season, provided enough late-inning relief to propel the Padres to the first pennant in their 16-year existence.

Subtract the losses from the wins, add that number to the total of saves, and the reality of Gossage's contribution becomes strikingly obvious; he gave the Padres a margin of 29 games that they did not enjoy previously.

"Without the Goose, we would not have been in first place," says Dick Williams, looking back on the '84 campaign. "Getting him gave us instant credibility. He provided an ingredient we lacked last year."

The father of two from Colorado Springs broke into pro ball in 1970 and reached the Chicago White Sox two years later, but didn't have his first big year until 1975. He won nine, saved 26, and posted a 1.98 ERA, but found himself shunted to a starter's role the following spring. After a 9–17 season for Paul Richards's last-place club, the Goose found himself packaged to Pittsburgh, along with lefty reliever Terry Forster, for hard-hitting outfielder Richie Zisk.

In 72 games—a career high—Gossage posted an 11–9 record, 1.62 ERA, and 26 saves under former White Sox pilot Chuck Tanner, then in his first year with the Pirates. But even the presence of Tanner, his first major league manager, wasn't enough to keep the Gossage from flying into the reentry draft. The New York Yankees, able to offer a much more lucrative contract than the Pirates, won the ensuing bidding war.

It was no coincidence that the Yankees finished first three times during the six years Gossage dominated their bullpen. In two of those three championship seasons, they advanced to the World Series.

TWO-PITCH STAR

During that time, Gossage built a reputation as a fireballing, intimidating reliever who depended on only two pitches: a blazing fastball and a fast curve that he called a "slurve." He glowered at enemy batters, worked like a man in a hurry to catch the 5:03 to Massapequa, and established himself as the most feared reliever in the game.

He had a career-high 33 saves in 1980 and a career-low 0.77 ERA in 1981, but Gossage was anything but pleased with his Yankee years. Frequent quarrels with the style and statements of George Steinbrenner, the controversial club owner, spoiled his stay in pinstripes.

"When I'd drive to Yankee Stadium, it was like driving to a funeral," he admitted later. "It seemed like when we won, we didn't get credit and when we lost, we got blamed. When you win and don't have any fun, something's wrong. Over

there, it seemed like we were working for nothing."

When his Yankee contract expired, The Goose was off and running. Atlanta, Toronto, and a host of other clubs begged and pleaded, but the twin attractions of the San Diego climate and potential championship club prevailed. By the All-Star break, the Padres realized they had pulled off a great coup.

ALL-STAR STATS

One of four relievers chosen for the National League's All-Star squad, Gossage brought a 4–2 record, 15 saves, and 2.90 ERA into the three-day midseason break. He added another save in the July 10 game, pitching the last inning of a 3–1 NL victory. With The Goose on the hill at chilly Candlestick Park, Eddie Murray fanned, pinch-hitter Don Mattingly flied out to left, Dave Winfield doubled, and Rickey Henderson struck out.

The eight-time All-Star, who now has 231 career saves, seems certain to reach the 300-save level before his San Diego contract runs out. Though Bruce Sutter is close, only Rollie Fingers has saved that many games lifetime.

"Every championship team has to have an ace and we finally got one," says Steve Garvey, the smiling slugger who anchors first base for San Diego. "He's been very much accepted, as a good man to have on and off the field."

Gossage has been instrumental in the development of fellow relievers Craig Lefferts and Dave Dravecky, lefthanders who teamed with righty Andy Hawkins to provide airtight middle relief in late-season and postseason play last year.

"He's tried to play down his role and give credit to others wherever possible," noted Phill Collier, the *San Diego Union* writer who has covered the club since its inception.

While the supporting cast deserves some recognition, it is The Goose who deserves most of the credit. Just ask his teammates.

TONY GWYNN
SAN DIEGO SURPRISE!

CAREER RECORD											
YEAR	CLUB	AVG.	G	AB	R	H	2B	3B	HR	RBI	SB
1978	Walla Walla, NW	.331	42	178	46	59	12	1	12	37	17
1981	Amarillo, TX	.462	23	91	22	42	8	2	4	19	5
1982	Hawaii	.328	93	366	65	120	23	2	5	46	14
1982	San Diego	.289	54	190	33	55	12	2	1	17	8
1983	Las Vegas, PCL	.342	17	73	15	25	8	0	0	7	3
1983	San Diego	.309	86	304	34	94	12	2	1	37	7
1984	San Diego	.351*	158	606	88	213	21	10	5	71	33

*—Led league

LEAGUE CHAMPIONSHIP SERIES RECORD										
YEAR	CLUB vs. OPP.	G	AB	R	H	RBI	2B	3B	HR	SB	BA
1984	San Diego vs. Chicago	5	19	6	7	3	2	0	0	0	.368

WORLD SERIES RECORD										
YEAR	CLUB vs. OPP.	G	AB	R	H	RBI	2B	3B	HR	SB	BA
1984	San Diego vs. Detroit	5	19	1	5	0	0	0	0	1	.263

When Tony Gwynn was five years old, he spent the better part of his days playing backyard wiffleball with older brother Charles. By the time Chris Gwynn, Tony's junior by five years, got to join them, the game had evolved into "sockball," utilizing old socks held together by rubber bands.

The socks had more durability than the plastic wiffle balls—and apparently more in common with real baseballs.

"By the time we got to Little League," Tony Gwynn remembers, "hitting a baseball was a piece of cake."

Things haven't changed for the lefthanded-hitting Californian; in 1984, his first full season in the major leagues, the 5-11, 185-pound outfielder hit .351 to lead the San Diego Padres to their first pennant. He led the world with 213 hits, as well as in average (both club records), and produced an impressive .410 on-base percentage, sharing two-league leadership with Gary Matthews of the Chicago Cubs and Eddie Murray of the Baltimore Orioles.

Baseball fans around the nation—who were barely familiar with his name and credentials when the 1984 season opened—won't forget his integral role in the come-from-behind victory engineered by the Padres in the National League Championship Series.

Seeking to become only the second club to rebound from a 2–0 deficit since the 1969 advent

Tony Gwynn hit .351 to win the National League batting title in his first full season.

of divisional play, the Padres scored late and often to take all three games at Jack Murphy Stadium in San Diego. Fittingly, Gwynn had the big hit.

FINISH WITH A FLOURISH

In the October 7 finale, the Cubs gave ace starter Rick Sutcliffe a 3–0 lead entering the home sixth inning. But the Padres scored twice, setting the stage for a seventh-inning comeback that starred Tony Gwynn.

Carmelo Martinez walked, moved to second on a sacrifice, and scored the tying run when a grounder by pinch-hitter Tim Flannery scooted through Bull Durham's legs at first base. Alan Wiggins singled to left, bringing Gwynn to the plate.

Using the typical inside-out swing that had terrorized National League pitchers all season, Gwynn ripped a bullet toward Ryne Sandberg, the league's best defensive second baseman. The ball was hit so hard that it took a wicked hop away from the Chicago infielder's outstretched glove. The lead run, followed by an insurance run, scored and Tony Gwynn wound up at second base. He then rode home on a Steve Garvey single.

"There's no question Tony Gwynn is the catalyst on our ballclub," says San Diego manager Dick Williams. "He makes things happen. He missed only a couple of games all season and that was because I wanted to rest him. He wants to play all the time, which is certainly a good example for any ball club.

"His value to us is much more than the league's highest average. He's willing to take a walk, lay down a bunt, or move a runner. He has excellent bat control and is willing to let Alan Wiggins run. He will take a strike or even two in order to give Wiggins time to make his move."

Williams, who had a Bert Campaneris-Bill North combination in Oakland and a Tim Raines-Rodney Scott tandem in Montreal, claims he's never had better table-setters than Wiggins and Gwynn.

"They're the best 1-2 punch I ever managed," he insists.

Davey Johnson, a rookie pilot with the Mets last year, agrees. "The keys for the Padres are the ability of Wiggins and Gwynn to get on base. When they lost the first two playoff games at Chicago, the Cubs kept them off base. But when they came back to San Diego, both Wiggins and Gwynn played well. That's why the Padres went to the World Series."

While poor pitching pulverized the Padres in the Fall Classic, Tony Gwynn maintained respectability; he hit .263 in the five-game debacle and threw in a stolen base for good measure.

UNKNOWN TALENT

Gwynn, who will turn 25 before the All-Star Game, had so little recognition before 1984 that high-priced free agent signee Goose Gossage, who left New York to ink a megabucks Padre pact, said he had never heard of him before arriving in San Diego.

Gwynn's bat changed all that; the nation's fans, entrusted with selecting starters for the All-Star Game, chose Gwynn, along with Dale Murphy and Darryl Strawberry, as starting outfielders. The San Diego sensation played left field, batted leadoff, and contributed one hit in three tries.

He was also voted a starting berth on the postseason All-Star team selected by the players for *The Sporting News*.

"Tony is in a class by himself," says San Diego batting coach Deacon Jones. "He knows the strike zone, he makes good contact, hits the ball to all fields, and has the speed to beat out infield hits. He likes to hit and he believes in himself. He takes an extra five minutes of batting practice every day and studies videotapes to detect any flaws.

"There isn't a pitcher in the league who wants Tony Gwynn up with a runner on third base. You know he'll make contact. He reminds me of Don Mueller, who used to be with the New York Giants when I was a kid. Mandrake the Magician. He'll get some funky hits and then he'll hit a line drive that you could hang three weeks' wash on."

The Padres are lucky to have Tony Gwynn; they almost lost him to pro basketball. Both San Diego clubs (the Clippers have since set sail for Los Angeles) drafted the San Diego State star on the same day. Though his favorite sport was basketball in high school at Long Beach, Gwynn decided he had a better future in professional baseball.

He signed with San Diego, which had picked him in the third round of the June 1981 draft of amateur free agents, and was assigned to Walla Walla, Washington, in the Northwest League. Wasting no time, Tony Gwynn gave hint of things to come by capturing the batting crown. Promoted to Amarillo, in the Double-A Texas League, he did even better, with a .462 mark in 23 games, and advanced to Triple-A Hawaii of the Pacific Coast League for 1982. He hit .328 there and reached the majors in time to play 54 games with the parent club that summer.

BAD BREAK

Targeted for a full season with the 1983 Padres, Gwynn's career took a detour; he suffered a fractured right wrist while playing in the Puerto Rican Winter League on December 30, 1982 and didn't reach the Padres (following a rehabilitation period with their new Triple-A team in Las Vegas) until June 21.

After a month of adjustment, Gwynn hit .333 from July 26 to season's end to wind up with an overall mark of .309. From August 11 through September 26, he hit safely in 39 of 41 games, including a club record 25-game hitting streak, longest in the National League that year.

"I just go up there, see the ball, and swing," he says. "I guess a lot of it is God-given ability. I remember reading Ted Williams's book *The Science of Hitting* once. It had all this stuff about hitting a certain number of pitches in a certain zone and you'd have this average. That's fine, but it's not for me. I just want to sit back on the ball and put it in play."

If he continues at his current levels, the San Diego rightfielder won't have to listen to Ted Williams. Or anyone else.

KEITH HERNANDEZ
MVP IN NUMBERS ONLY

CAREER RECORD

YEAR	CLUB	AVG.	G	AB	R	H	2B	3B	HR	RBI	SB
1972	St. Petersburg	.256	84	309	38	79	16	5	5	41	6
1972	Tulsa	.241	11	29	5	7	1	0	0	1	0
1973	Arkansas	.260	105	388	62	101	20	2	3	52	8
1973	Tulsa	.333	31	120	20	40	6	1	5	25	0
1974	Tulsa	.351	102	353	67	124	18	6	14	63	0
1974	St. Louis	.294	14	34	3	10	1	2	0	2	0
1975	St. Louis	.250	64	188	20	47	8	2	3	20	0
	Tulsa	.330	85	324	70	107	29	3	10	48	3
1976	St. Louis	.289	129	374	54	108	21	5	7	46	4
1977	St. Louis	.291	161	560	90	163	41	4	15	91	7
1978	St. Louis	.255	159	542	90	138	32	4	11	64	13
1979	St. Louis	.344	161	610	116	210	48	11	11	105	11
1980	St. Louis	.321	159	595	111	191	39	8	16	99	14
1981	St. Louis	.306	103	376	65	115	27	4	8	48	12
1982	St. Louis	.299	160	579	79	173	33	6	7	94	19
1983	St. Louis	.297	150	538	77	160	23	7	12	63	9
	New York, NL										
1984	New York, NL	.311	154	550	83	171	31	0	15	94	2

LEAGUE CHAMPIONSHIP SERIES RECORD

YEAR	CLUB vs. OPP.	AVG.	G	AB	R	H	2B	3B	HR	RBI	SB
1982	St. Louis vs. Atlanta	.333	3	12	3	4	0	0	0	1	0

WORLD SERIES RECORD

YEAR	CLUB vs. OPP.	AVG.	G	AB	R	H	2B	3B	HR	RBI	SB
1982	St. Louis vs. Milwaukee	.259	7	27	4	7	2	0	1	8	0

Had the New York Mets finished first instead of second in the National League East in 1984, both Most Valuable Players might have been named Hernandez.

Willie Hernandez, the lefthanded screwball specialist who became the ace reliever of the World Champion Detroit Tigers, won the American League's award, while Keith Hernandez (no rela-tion) was piling up MVP numbers for the Mets.

"He's my Rock of Gilbraltar," says New York manager Dave Johnson of the hard-hitting first baseman. "Even though I see him day after day, I still marvel at the plays he makes. I just can't count the ways he has contributed to the success and uplifting of the Mets. He's to first base what Brooks Robinson was to third base—and every time we need a two-out clutch hit, he always comes through. There's a feeling on our bench: stay close in the late innings and Keith will find a way."

With a .409 on-base percentage, he ranked only a point behind major-league leaders Gary Matthews, Tony Gwynn, and Eddie Murray; his 17 game-winning runs batted in and 97 walks ranked second to Matthews in the National League; he ranked seventh in batting at .311, the fourth time he's topped .300 in nine full seasons; and his 94 RBI were only 12 behind league-leaders Gary Carter and Mike Schmidt (Hernandez has had four previous seasons of at least 90 RBI).

FLAWLESS FIELDER

The six-time winner of a Gold Glove for fielding excellence also contributed 15 homers—one of four Mets to hit at least that many—and played in his third All-Star Game, even though fans voting for the team chose the better-known Steve Garvey as the National League starter at first base. The players reversed that oversight by choosing Hernandez for the post-season All-Star team in *The Sporting News*.

Even when he shared National League MVP honors with Willie Stargell in 1979, Hernandez was not selected to start the All-Star Game. Every time he has made the team, he's been a substitute.

"That's incredible," says pitcher Ed Lynch, a teammate on the 1984 Mets. "The fans just don't know everything Keith does for a team. He's a field general. He's on you on every pitch. He leads the league in going to the mound and it's always to remind you of something important. He knows something about every hitter in the league. The game is fun to Keith and that enthusiasm spreads."

It was no fun for Hernandez on June 15, 1983, the day the St. Louis Cardinals, his first major-league team, traded him to the Mets for pitchers Neil Allen and Rick Ownbey. The 6-0, 195-pound lefthanded hitter felt he was going from contender to clunker. But that was before he got a good look at Darryl Strawberry, Hubie Brooks, Jesse Orosco, and some of the other young players whose skills seemed about to blossom.

In February 1984, Hernandez abandoned thoughts of demanding a trade or seeking free agency; he inked a five-year contract with the Mets that will carry him through the 1989 season. Having him around will save numerous errors for the rest of the New York infield.

Though he was originally unhappy about his trade from the St. Louis Cardinals to the Mets, Hernandez has developed into the veteran leader of a young, hungry club. A dangerous clutch hitter who produced a .409 on-base percentage last year, he was runner-up to Chicago-s Ryne Sandberg in the NL Most Valuable Player poll.

"My dad used to take me to Candlestick Park to watch Bill White when I was a kid," Hernandez recalls. "His express purpose for taking me was so I could watch Bill play first base and then practice doing everything he did."

Hernandez, a master at digging balls out of the dirt, learned his lessons well.

MR. DEPENDABILITY

"It gave me confidence every time a ground ball is hit to me that Keith was over there," says

Hubie Brooks, the Mets' shortstop who was swapped to Montreal last December.

"He gets to balls Dave Kingman wouldn't have a chance of reaching. *No* first baseman can scoop the balls Keith picks up."

When he joined the Mets, Hernandez supplanted Kingman at the bag. Before the 1984 season had started, Kingman was given his outright release, paving the way for his signing by the Oakland Athletics as a designated hitter (a DH does not have to field).

"Sometimes a manager wants to get some guy's bat into the lineup and figures he can hide him at first base," Hernandez suggests. "But he's going to have to produce a lot offensively if he can't field his position. You can lose a lot of games if you don't have a good first baseman."

Errors are not the true measure of a first baseman, according to Hernandez. Assists are the key. "If you don't get a lot of assists, it means you don't have a lot of range," he says.

Unlike Steve Garvey, who failed to commit an error last year but is encumbered with such an unreliable arm that opposing teams try to make him throw, Hernandez has complete confidence in every aspect of his game. Fielding statistics are virtually ignored by the media, but baseball insiders and fans who see him know about the defensive capabilities of Hernandez.

He's no Mike Squires, though; Hernandez is both a defensive and offensive generator—as well as the recognized team leader by both teammates and fans.

GOOD TEAM PLAYER

"In measuring his value to our team, you have to go beyond statistics," insists Dave Johnson. "He's the consummate professional and he transmits that professionalism to our younger players.

Off the field, he holds the team together. He keeps everyone laughing on those long road trips. He's one of the guys and the players like him. And he always has the right thing to say to the media."

Looking back on the almost-but-not-quite 1984 season, Hernandez describes the first month as "the most fun I've ever had in my life."

"I felt it every time I got in a cab or passed the doorman at my condominium," says Hernandez, one of the few Mets who lives in Manhattan. "Everybody was telling me, 'Thank you, keep it up, you're making my nights.' They all said they were long-time Mets' fans who waited years for the team to start winning. It was great."

The native Californian, a history buff who translates his knowledge of Civil War subjects into paintings of famous generals, came to the major leagues almost as an afterthought. He was drafted by the Cardinals on the 40th round of the June 1971 draft of amateur free agents.

Three years later, at the end of the season, he got his first taste of big-league pitching. By 1976, his appetite had grown accustomed to it and he was in the majors to stay. The Mets are glad they got him—a deal made possible only because of bad feelings between Hernandez and fiery St. Louis manager Whitey Herzog.

"I used to think Wes Parker was the best first baseman I'd ever see," says Bobby Valentine, who coached third for the Mets last year, "but I've changed my mind. I even told Parker that Keith is the best. What Keith does better than anyone is play so far off the line that he can cut off balls in the hole. I'd love to have a dollar for every time I've heard someone say, 'Keith's the only guy who can make that play.'"

Says Dave Johnson of the lifetime .300 hitter: "If Whitey Herzog has any more like Hernandez that he wants to trade, tell him to call me."

Don't hold your breath, Dave; there aren't any more like Hernandez anywhere.

WILLIE HERNANDEZ
MOTOWN'S BULLPEN MAGICIAN

CAREER RECORD

YEAR	CLUB	W-L	ERA	G	GS	CG	ShO	SV	IP	H	BB	SO
1974	Spartanburg	11-11	2.75	26	26*	13*	1	0	190*	169	49	179*
1975	Reading	8-2	2.97	13	11	7	1	0	91	79	25	46
	Toledo	6-4	3.28	13	13	4	0	0	80	86	26	46
1976	Oklahoma City	8-9	4.52	25	23	3	1	0	135	154	30	88
1977	Chicago, NL	8-7	3.03	67	1	0	0	4	110	94	28	78
1978	Chicago, NL	8-2	3.75	54	0	0	0	3	60	57	35	38
1979	Chicago, NL	4-4	5.01	51	2	0	0	0	79	85	39	53
1980	Chicago, NL	1-9	4.42	53	7	0	0	0	108	115	45	75
1981	Iowa	4-5	3.89	18	8	2	0	2	74	84	27	41
	Chicago, NL	0-0	3.86	12	0	0	0	2	14	14	8	13
1982	Chicago, NL	4-6	3.00	75	0	0	0	10	75	74	24	54
1983	Chicago, NL/Philadelphia	9-4	3.28	74	1	0	0	8	115.1	109	32	93
1984	Detroit	9-3	1.92	80*		0	0	32	140.1	96	36	112

*—Led league

LEAGUE CHAMPIONSHIP SERIES RECORD

YEAR	CLUB vs. OPP.	W-L	ERA	G	CG	ShO	SV	IP	H	BB	SO
1984	Detroit vs. Kansas City	0-0	2.25	2	0	0	1	4	3	1	3

WORLD SERIES RECORD

YEAR	CLUB vs. OPP.	W-L	ERA	G	CG	ShO	SV	IP	H	BB	SO
1983	Philadelphia vs. Baltimore	0-0	0.00	3	0	40	0	0	0	1	4
1984		0-0	0.00	3	0	0	2	5.1	4	0	0

As he prepared for spring training with the Chicago Cubs in 1982, Willie Hernandez knew he'd have to perform well to keep his job as a middle-innings relief pitcher. He'd done so little to distinguish himself in four previous seasons with Chicago that he'd spent most of 1981 in the minors—an embarrassing demotion for a player on a pitching-poor team.

The sinking fastball and slider Hernandez threw had become all too familiar to National League hitters; he lost nine out of ten decisions during the 1980 campaign. To make matters worse, he was only marginally more effective in Triple-A a year later.

Though his statistics were howling for help, Hernandez didn't know where to turn—until he met fellow Latin lefthander Mike Cuellar in Bayamon, Puerto Rico.

Hernandez, a native Puerto Rican, was working his way into shape, while Cuellar, a one-time

Willie Hernandez escaped his former role as a middle reliever in the National League to become the only reliever ever to win Cy Young and MVP honors in the same season.

Baltimore star from Cuba, was assigned to coaching some younger players. As it turned out, none of those youngsters profited as much from the coaching as Willie Hernandez.

It was at Bayamon that Cuellar introduced Hernandez to the screwball.

"Mike showed me how to grip the ball, how to set my wrist at an angle for the screwball," Hernandez remembers. "In spring training, Billy Connors set my motion for the pitch."

The 6-2, 185-pound southpaw responded with a 4–6 record, his first 10-save season, and a 3.00 earned run average in a career-high 75 games. He also opened the eyes of observers all around the majors. On May 23, 1983, the Phillies traded for him and less than a year later, on March 24, 1984, he went to Detroit.

Philadelphia was willing to let him go because it coveted the righthanded bats and versatility of John Wockenfuss and Glenn Wilson—and because Al Holland, another lefty, was coming off a big year in relief.

CHANGE OF VENUE

But Detroit envisioned a new role for Hernandez—late-inning stopper—while the Phils failed to realize that Holland couldn't handle that function without a strong middleman to set him up. Hernandez, who played that role for Philadelphia, blossomed in Detroit when bullpen sidekick Aurelio Lopez proved adept at the former Hernandez function. Together, the left-right Tiger tandem had a 19-4 record and 46 saves, giving them a direct hand in 65 of Detroit's 104 victories.

"Our bullpen helped me win 17 games," says Milt Wilcox, who failed to pitch a complete game last year. "I did my job and they did theirs."

Hernandez was the key to the success of the relief corps; working 80 games, the most in Tiger history, he had a 9-3 record, 1.92 earned run average, and 32 saves in 33 save opportunities—plus a save in the Championship Series and two more in the World Series. He was on the mound at the end of the September 18 divisional title clincher, the October 4 playoff finale, and the October 14 World Series finale.

"Willie knows when he enters a game he's either going to win it, save it, or strike someone out," says Roger Craig, who retired as Detroit pitching coach at the end of last season. "I was a player and coach for 35 years and I've never seen a pitcher dominate the game as much as he has."

The record of the 1984 season supports that thesis. When the Tigers won 35 of their first 40 games, the fastest start in baseball history, Hernandez was quite ordinary, with seven saves and a 3.03 ERA—45 points higher than the team's 2.58 at the same point.

As the Tigers divided their next 40 games, however, their team ERA was 4.34, a far cry above the 1.47 Hernandez recorded in his one-man effort to keep the pitching staff afloat. The 29-year-old southpaw had three victories and eight saves over that streak, earning his first All-Star designation in the process.

COOL UNDER FIRE

"Pressure doesn't bother me," says Hernandez, explaining his success. "Batters have pressure too, so that makes it even. They're under pressure to get a hit, just as I am to get an out. I could pitch 162 games a year if I faced only one or two batters a game. The worst I felt all year was when I got too much rest. Three days of not pitching and I don't feel so good, so I throw on the sidelines. If I miss two days in a row, my arm gets weak."

That attitude sits well with Tiger manager Sparky Anderson, whose penchant for pulling starters quickly earned him the nickname Captain Hook during his long tenure in Cincinnati. Anderson had a single 20-game-winning starter but four 25-save relievers during his nine years with the Reds.

Hernandez called his new manager the night of the trade and told him he needed a steady diet of work to be effective.

"When he told me he liked to pitch a lot, I said, 'You've come to the right house and knocked on the right door,'" Anderson remembers. "When he reported to work the next day, he asked me how much he was going to pitch. I said, 'As much as you want—80, 90 games.'

"Before the trade, we had him scouted very well. I got a full report from Tony Perez (a Hernandez teammate with Philadelphia in 1983). Tony told me Willie won the pennant for the Phillies—that he took them to the ninth inning when Al Holland took over. I got carried away. I had to have Hernandez but I was worried something would go wrong during the negotiations and the trade wouldn't go through."

TORONTO'S LOSS

Toronto, the runner-up to Detroit in the American League East last year, was also after Hernan-

dez—but balked when the Phils asked for hard-hitting young outfielder Jesse Barfield in return.

"If the Blue Jays had him instead of us, we might have finished 10 games behind them," Anderson says.

Toronto turned down the chance to land Hernandez because it paid too much attention to past history; the crafty lefthander took a career total of 27 saves into the 1984 season. That's not much for seven seasons in the big leagues, though statistics for middle relievers are misleading (to qualify for a save, a relief pitcher must finish the game, as well as meeting several other criteria).

Hernandez, armed with a screwball that tails away from righthanded hitters (confounding the left-right strategy employed by most managers in the late innings), finished 68 games and failed in a save situation only in the 160th game, on September 28 at New York. He retired both batters he faced but allowed one of them to drive home the tying run with a sacrifice fly. Detroit eventually won in 12 innings but Hernandez had lost his bid for a perfect season.

He didn't lose when the writers voted for postseason awards, however; he joined Rollie Fingers of the 1981 Milwaukee Brewers as the only relievers to win the Cy Young and Most Valuable Player awards in the same season.

With 12 first-place votes, seven seconds, and seven thirds, Hernandez edged Kansas City's Dan Quisenberry in Cy Young voting that produced the first 1–2 finish by relievers in baseball history. He had an easier time in MVP balloting, finishing with 306 points, well ahead of the 247 polled by runner-up Kent Hrbek.

"We're not exactly the best team to fall behind against," says Alan Trammell, summing up the sensational season of the newest Tiger. "We've got that big guy to close the door."

KENT HRBEK
LOCAL BOY MAKES GOOD

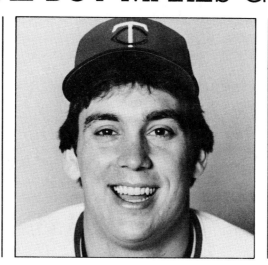

		CAREER RECORD									
YEAR	CLUB	AVG.	G	AB	R	H	2B	3B	HR	RBI	SB
1979	Elizabethton	.203	17	59	5	12	2	0	1	11	2
1980	Wisconsin Rapids	.267	115	419	74	112	16	0	19	76	1
1981	Visalia	.379	121	462	119	175	25	5	27	111	12
	Minnesota	.239	24	67	5	16	5	0	1	7	0
1982	Minnesota	.301	140	532	82	160	21	4	23	92	3
1983	Minnesota	.297	141	515	75	153	41	5	16	84	4
1984	Minnesota	.311	149	559	80	174	31	3	27	107	1

In 1978, when Calvin Griffith was still operating the Minnesota Twins on a shoe-string budget, a loyal employee from his concessions department told the owner about a talented kid prospect at Kennedy High School.

Griffith packed his rather considerable girth into his automobile, motored over to the school, and personally scouted the local slugger. He liked what he saw—in a vague sort of way—but he also liked the idea that the kid just might overcome the odds and become a hometown hero.

Under Griffith's orders, the Twins drafted negotiating rights to the prospect—in the 17th round of the amateur free agent draft in June 1978. Two years later, the power potential was beginning to show and, by 1981, the minor-league numbers were too big to ignore.

Kent Hrbek, called to Minnesota, made his first major-league homer a big one—a 12th-inning blast to beat the New York Yankees. In 1982, as the everyday first baseman on a struggling team,

he was an American League All-Star, a .300 hitter, and a strong challenger to Baltimore's Cal Ripken, Jr., for Rookie-of-the-Year honors.

The 6-4, 225-pound Minneapolis native, a resident of nearby Excelsior, was even more devastating as the leader of the Twins' revival in 1984. His .311 batting average and 107 runs batted in led the team, he tied Tom Brunansky for club leadership with 11 game-winning RBI, and he hit 27 home runs to rank second to Brunansky's 32 among the Twins.

MVP BRIDESMAID

Clearly the leader of a team that finished in a second-place tie, three games behind, Hrbek capped his season with a second-place finish in the voting for the American League's Most Valuable Player award. He had five first-place votes, seven seconds, and 10 thirds to amass 247 votes,

The Hubert H. Humphrey Metrodome, one of two covered parks in the American League, is conducive to the long drives of Kent Hrbek, a local boy who made good.

second only to the 306 of Detroit reliever Willie Hernandez.

"I play the game like a little man," says Hrbek, explaining one of the factors that entranced the MVP electors. "I dive for ground balls, I go hard into second base. You don't see a lot of big men playing that way."

A good bunter who's rarely called upon for the sacrifice, Hrbek thrives on high, tight fastballs and off-speed deliveries, and is a selective hitter when he's going well (over-anxiety during slumps causes him to jump on the first ball frequently). A pull hitter with more power against righties than lefties, the lefthanded-hitting, righthanded-throwing Hrbek hits with power to right field but often hammers hard drives to left.

When he's hot, the Minnesota mauler is almost unstoppable. Consider his statistics for July: a .368 average, .717 slugging percentage, 10 homers, and 31 runs batted in over a 27-game span.

During one eight-game streak, he went 16-for-33 with three homers, five doubles, and 10 RBI to raise his batting average to .329, third in the league. On July 7—three days before the All-Star Game—his .333 was second, trailing only Dave Winfield, but he wasn't among the American League All-Stars.

The fans, in their infinite wisdom, had given him only 251,150 votes, seventh among first basemen, and chose as their starter at the position California's Rod Carew, a mere shadow of his former self—but a name more recognizable than Kent Hrbek.

"I don't worry about hitting for the All-Stars,"

said Hrbek at the time. "I just worry about hitting for the Twins."

He shouldn't have to worry; in two of his three Minnesota summers, he's topped .300 and exceeded 90 RBI. And he's never hit less than 16 home runs in a season.

YOUNG AND HUNGRY

Such statistics satisfy team officials who insisted that the best way to restore the championship seasons of 1969 and 1970 (when the Twins topped the American League West) is to build with young players. The team stayed in contention for the title until the final weekend last year.

"We're having the times of our lives," Hrbek says. "We're a great bunch of guys who didn't feel any pressure being in the race because it was the most fun any of us ever had. Back when I was getting all the credit and we were losing, that wasn't any fun at all."

Hrbek believes that having fun helps keep a team loose and promotes productivity on the field. Exploiting the happy-team-is-a-winning-team philosophy has become a personal passion for Kent Hrbek.

He was one of the instigators behind the creation of The Hood, an unsightly mask which must be carried around by the Minnesota player who has struck out three times in a game most recently. The mask is appropriately dubbed with the initials "K-K-K."

Hrbek is also the man who started the clubhouse fan club for The Claw (Baron Von Raschke), a noteworthy Twin Cities wrestler who is often the center of attraction when players gather in the Metrodome clubhouse to watch television.

Members of the Twins often wear T-shirts depicting The Claw and other local wrestlers. The shirts, distributed by Hrbek, are invisible to fans, since they're under the uniform jerseys, but the clubhouse is a place for dressing, undressing and wise-cracking.

"The thing I like about these guys," says Billy Gardner, the only manager who sells meat during the off-season, "is that they're loose in the clubhouse but all business on the field."

That's especially true for Hrbek, who carried the club all year—offensively and defensively.

DYNAMIC DEFENDER

"He should win a Gold Glove," says the manager of the first baseman. "The only thing that can keep it from him is the lack of attention he's received so far. He's the best all-around first baseman in our league and I can't imagine there's a better first baseman in the National League. He's also one of the best hitters in the league and he's going to get better."

Gardner insists Hrbek is the best first baseman he's seen during his long career. "He reacts to situations like he's been around for 10 years," the manager says. "Put it all together and he's the best first baseman I've seen in 39 years."

The manager is actually the beneficiary of a mother's advice to her son. Early last year, Tina Hrbek, who never misses a Minnesota home game, corrected a Kent Hrbek slump.

"I noticed he was dropping his elbow and shoulder," she recalls. "Because of that, he was just pushing the ball. I told him if he brought his arm up a little, he might get more punch. It worked."

Mrs. Hrbek has seen about 90 percent of her son's games, from scholastic baseball to the majors, but says she's surprised he became a ballplayer—even though he gave hint of his future size when he came home from the hospital as a nine-pound, three-ounce baby.

"I should take Mom on the road as my roomie," laughs Hrbek, who earned $375,000 last year—a tidy sum for an eligible bachelor. He won't qualify for possible free agency until the fall of 1987, but the goal of the off-season was to secure a lucrative, long-term pact that would give both player and team a firm foundation for the future.

For Kent Hrbek, who turns 25 on May 21, that future glows with enormous promise.

DAVE KINGMAN
KING OF CLOUT

CAREER RECORD

YEAR	CLUB	AVG.	G	AB	R	H	2B	3B	HR	RBI	SB
1970	Amarillo	.295	60	210	41	62	9	1	15	41	3
1971	Phoenix	.278	105	392	89	109	29	5	26	99	11
	San Francisco	.278	41	115	17	32	10	2	6	24	5
1972	San Francisco	.225	135	472	65	106	17	4	29	83	16
1973	San Francisco	.203	112	305	54	62	10	1	24	55	8
1974	San Francisco	.223	121	350	41	78	18	2	18	55	8
1975	New York, NL	.231	134	502	65	116	22	1	36	88	7
1976	New York, NL	.238	123	474	70	113	14	1	37	86	7
1977	New York, NL San Diego	.222	114	379	38	84	16	0	20	67	5
	California; New York, NL	.217	18	60	9	13	4	0	6	11	
1978	Chicago, NL	.266	119	395	65	105	17	4	28	79	3
1979	Chicago, NL	.288	145	532	97	153	19	5	48	115	4
1980	Chicago, NL	.278	81	255	31	71	8	0	18	57	2
1981	New York, NL	.221	100	353	40	78	11	3	22	59	6
1982	New York, NL	.204	149	535	80	109	9	1	37	99	4
1983	New York, NL	.198	100	248	25	49	7	0	13	29	2
1984	Oakland	.268	147	549	68	147	23	1	35	118	2

*—Led league

LEAGUE CHAMPIONSHIP SERIES RECORD

YEAR	CLUB vs. OPP.	AVG.	G	AB	R	H	2B	3B	HR	RBI
1971	San Francisco vs. Pittsburgh	.111	4	9	0	1	0	0	0	0

PITCHING RECORD

YEAR	CLUB	W-L	ERA	G	IP	Pct	H	BB	SO
1973	San Francisco	0-0	9.00	2	4	.000	3	6	4

Whatever goes up must come down. Well, not necessarily.

Dave Kingman voided that basic law of physics last May 4 at the Hubert H. Humphrey Metrodome in Minneapolis. In a game against the Minnesota Twins, the giant designated hitter of the Oakland Athletics hit a 187-foot pop fly above the pitcher's mound. The ball disappeared into a seven-inch hole in the fiberglass liner of the stadium's dome and Jim Evans, chief of the bewildered umpiring crew, awarded Kingman a "roof-rule" double.

The next night, the Minnesota ground crew came up empty in a search for the original ball.

"He can reach places other hitters can't," says former Oakland teammate Davey Lopes (now with the Cubs) of Kingman. "Nobody can hit a ball as high and deep as he can."

Kingman's clouts earned him American League Comeback-of-the-Year honors; he hit 35 homers, including three in an April 16 contest at the Seattle Kingdome.

Though knee problems probably held down his numbers, Kingman took rival pitchers high and deep 35 times in 1984. Only Boston's Tony Armas, who hit 43, homered more often among American Leaguers. Kingman also had 118 runs batted in, trailing only Armas (123) and his Boston teammate Jim Rice (122).

Comeback-of-the-Year honors were showered on the powerful righthanded hitter, who now needs just 28 home runs to reach 400 lifetime. Those citations were richly deserved after Kingman rebounded from a sour '83 campaign in which the New York Mets gave him only 37 at-bats over the second half. With Oakland, where Kingman signed as a free agent walk-on during spring training, the 6-6, 210-pound slugger lifted his batting average from .198 to .268, 34 points above his lifetime mark. Basking in the new-found appreciation of teammates, management, and fans, Kingman also shed his image as a truck-

driver in pinstripes—a man who would run you over first and ask questions later.

The Sporting News summed up the change in a headline announcing Kingman's selection as the winner of American League comeback honors: KONG FINDS HAPPINESS IN OAKLAND.

GAMBLE PAYS OFF

Only a severe power shortage, plus a willingness to overlook past problems, convinced the Athletics to take a flyer on the two-time National League home run king, regarded as over-the-hill or not worth the risk by the other clubs in the majors.

After the end of the 1983 season, Kingman thought he would be traded by the Mets, who had acquired All-Star Keith Hernandez from the Cardinals to play first base. With no designated hitter in the National League and no room (or desire) for Kingman to play the outfield, New York had to make a move. But who would want a moody 35-year-old with a $675,000-a-year contract and no true defensive position?

The Seattle Mariners thought about it—until they obtained Gorman Thomas and Barry Bonnell in separate swaps.

Several Japanese teams showed interest—but Kingman put them on hold pending developments with teams in the American major leagues. Agent David Landfield was instructed to let the teams come to him. Oakland finally did—calling Kingman at his off-season home in South Lake Tahoe, near the California-Nevada border.

An instant spring training success in the high, dry air of Arizona, Kingman won a contract calling for $40,000, the major-league minimum. Under baseball law, the Mets were obligated to honor the balance of his guaranteed salary under Kingman's existing multi-year contract.

Kingman turned out to be quite a bargain. He hit 10 homers in April—one short of the big-league record shared by Mike Schmidt, Graig Nettles, and Willie Stargell—and had a .606 average with eight homers and 19 RBI over one nine-game road trip.

INDOOR FIREWORKS

His biggest game came on April 16, in the Seattle Kingdome. The newly minted Oakland star slammed three home runs—two two-run shots and a grand slam—to become the second player in the West Coast history of the franchise to enjoy a three-homer game (Reggie Jackson did it on July 2, 1969, against the Seattle Pilots).

It was Kingman's fifth three-homer game and third eight-RBI game. The grand slam, the 12th of his career, was one of three he delivered for the 1984 Athletics, making him the leader in that category among active players.

"We got him for his power, no question about that," said batting coach Billy Williams early last year. "He's accepted the challenge. He knows what he can do and what we want him to do. He has the ability to lead the league in home runs and a lot of other things too."

Had he not suffered early-season ligament damage that limited him to 146 games and required him to wear a light knee brace, Kingman might have made Williams sound like a prophet.

"He enjoyed himself," said Williams, summarizing the season. "He was probably telling the Mets, 'I'm not finished.' And he's probably asking himself, 'Where has the designated hitter been all my life?' "

Kingman played only a few games at first base—Oakland manager Steve Boros and his successor, Jackie Moore, decided playing defense would put pressure on him—and concentrated on winning friends and influencing people through the social graces and the strength of his bat.

He hosted a barbecue for the team near the end of spring training and maintained year-long good relations with the four Bay Area writers who traveled with the team.

"I'm enjoying this season more than any of my others because of the people I'm working with," he said in July.

MEETING THE CHALLENGE

"I liked the challenge of going to spring training and having to make the team. I wanted to put some good numbers on the board because my contract ran out after the 1984 season. I have a lot of pride and want to fulfill my contract."

Kingman pointed out that he could have collected a fat salary from the Mets even if he had stayed on his boat and fished Lake Tahoe all summer. He had something to prove and he did—though Baltimore manager Joe Altobelli, charged with selecting the American League All-Stars, bypassed Kingman, then the league leader in homers (23) and one of the leaders in RBI (71).

Kingman spent the All-Star break fishing, backpacking, and enjoying his boat—while the American Leaguers who went to the game fanned 11 times in a 3–1 defeat at San Francisco's Candlestick Park. Had he been selected, Kingman would have been a hometown hero at the All-Star Game.

"If that's the way they pick their All-Star team, no wonder they lose so much," he says. "That was definitely a motivating factor for me. But (Seattle general manager) Hal Keller started it all. He said I was a mistake hitter. Well, I have now hit 377 mistakes!

"It's the little things that irritate you. They mount up. You sit down, you're tired, you start to think, and your blood pressure starts going up. Then you go out and hit."

Kingman got into shape for the season by dropping 15 pounds—"I decided quickness was more important than strength," he says. Now in his 15th season, the veteran of seven major-league teams seeks his fourth All-Star appointment, his first World Series appearance, and his first Most Valuable Player Award. If he keeps his bat hot and his temper cool, all seem to be within his reach.

MARK LANGSTON
INSTANT STRIKEOUT CHAMP

		CAREER RECORD								
YEAR	CLUB	W-L	ERA	G	CG	ShO	SV	IP	H	BB	SO
1981	Bellingham	7-3	3.39	13	5	1	0	85.0	81	46	97
1982	Bakersfield	12-7	2.54	26	7	3	0	177.0	143	102	161
1983	Chattanooga	14-9	3.59	28	10	0	0	198.0	187	102	142
1984	Seattle	17-10	3.40	35	5	2	0	225	188	118	204

Who says quality young lefthanded pitchers are an endangered species? In Seattle, they seem to grow on trees.

In 1982, the Mariners came up with Ed Vande Berg, a relief pitcher who worked in 78 games, a rookie record. A year later, Matt Young made the American League All-Star team as a rookie. And last year, Bud Black—traded to Kansas City by the Mariners on October 23, 1981—joined Mark Langston as two of the top pitchers in the American League.

Mark who?

"It's a dream, that's what it is," says the 24-year-old San Diego native of his 17–10 season for a 74–88 team. "You don't want to let it sink in. I just try to do my job."

The one-time surfer from San Diego State jumped from Chattanooga to Seattle without stopping at the Triple-A level—a move roughly parallel with going from peanut farmer to President. It happens, but not often.

Also in that category is a rookie winning a strikeout title; the last time an American Leaguer did it was in 1955, when Herb Score whiffed 245 for the Cleveland Indians. Never before had rookies led *both* leagues in strikeouts in one season until Langston, with 204, and teenage tornado Dwight Gooden perfected the parlay in 1984.

With Seattle in need of pitching help, Del Crandall gave Langston the chance to win a job in spring training. The 6-2, 177-pound southpaw was never headed. The only Seattle starter not to miss a start, Langston went from good to sensational as the weather turned warmer.

After the All-Star break, he was 11–3 with a 2.98 earned run average, including seven straight wins and a 2.20 ERA for the month of August. He ended that month with a 12-strikeout, 5–1 victory over Detroit—the league's top run-scoring team. The Tigers managed two hits—none after the second inning.

The Detroit outing was one of two 12-strikeout games for Langston; he also whiffed 11 once en route to a season that produced the most victories by a rookie southpaw since Gary Peters took 19 with the 1963 White Sox.

SUMMER SUCCESS

In July, August, and September, Langston won four games each. He was American League Player-of-the-Week for the period June 25–July 1, following back-to-back shutouts (the first in Mariners' history) over the White Sox and Red Sox. He set club marks for wins, winning percentage (.630), consecutive wins, consecutive strikeouts (7), consecutive shutout innings (21), and—oops—walks. Not bad work for a pitcher who had only two wins heading into June and lots of reasons to think his team might be planning to get him that missing Triple-A experience in the near future.

Buoyed by a 91-mile-per-hour fastball, a slow curve, and a veteran's knack for changing speeds, Langston thrived on a friendly competition with Seattle staff ace Jim Beattie.

"I watch Zelmo do it, then I want to top him," Langston laughs. "I watch Jim throw and then I try to do the same things he does."

On July 1, for example, Langston fired a 1–0 three-hitter at the Boston Red Sox—the night after Beattie had throttled the hard-hitting Bosox with a six-hit, 2–1 decision.

"What's so impressive about Langston," says Ralph Houk, who managed the Red Sox last year before opting for retirement, "is that he changes speeds extremely well for a youngster."

Langston himself credits his slow curve—a pitch he calls the jukeball—for helping him win American League Rookie Pitcher-of-the-Year designation from *The Sporting News*.

He was throwing it in the bullpen before a May start when Frank Funk, then the Seattle pitching coach, took notice. Ordered to throw it in a game, Langston fanned nine in $7\frac{2}{3}$ innings against Baltimore May 29.

RAVES OF A RIVAL

"Mark Langston is the very best pitcher I've seen since I came into the American League," insists Sparky Anderson, who took over as manager of the Detroit Tigers early in the 1979 campaign. "He's the best lefthander I've seen in 15 years in the big leagues—and I thought Dave Righetti was special. This guy is something else."

Anderson's syntax is often saturated with superlatives, but the manager's message has much significance.

Last August 20, Langston's 24th birthday, the pitcher treated himself to his 10th win in his last 14 decisions with an 11-strikeout performance against Sparky Anderson's eventual World Cham-

Lefty Mark Langston bypassed the Triple-A level en route to the American League's strikeout crown as a 1984 rookie. Langston and Dwight Gooden of the New York Mets both won 17 games in 1984 as they became the first pair of freshmen to lead both leagues in whiffs in one season.

pions. In the winning clubhouse after the game, Langston told reporters, "Last year, being here wasn't even on my mind. My only goal was to stick up here all year. I guess I did it, huh?"

The 1983 Southern League All-Star—Chattanooga's leader in wins, starts, completions, innings, and strikeouts—started slowly for Seattle, splitting his first 16 decisions and posting a so-so 3.65 earned run mark. But he showed promise of better things to come with 87 strikeouts in 80⅔ innings pitched.

By the date of his birthday, he had 151 strikeouts, two behind American League leader Mike Witt of the California Angels. Both pitchers finished strong—Witt with a 10-strikeout, 1–0 perfect game against the Texas Rangers and Langston with a nine-strikeout, 5–3 triumph over the Chicago White Sox—as the battle for strikeout leadership narrowed to a three-man race. At the end, Langston led Toronto's Dave Stieb by six and Witt by eight (the race might have been tighter if Witt had made one more start to equalize the numbers of games started by the three pitchers at 35 each).

QUICK PROMOTION

The Santa Clara, California resident reached the Mariners after a relatively brief minor-league tenure of three seasons. He broke into pro ball at Bellingham, Washington of the Northwest League in 1981 after the Mariners made him their third-round pick in the June draft of amateur free agents. The talented southpaw immediately won seven of ten decisions and averaged more than a strikeout an inning, working his way up the minor-league ladder, first to Bakersfield and then to Chattanooga. His only problem along the way has been an occasional bout of wildness.

Even though he led the Seattle staff with 118 walks last year, Langston won three more games than Mike Parrott, who had held the club record for wins in a season (with a 14–12 record in 1979). Matt Young had held the team mark for wins by a rookie, based upon his 11–15 log in 1983.

The highlight, in Langston's memory, was the season finale. As he walked off the field with his 17th win and the strikeout title intact, the freshman star was showered with confetti. "This is it, this is the max," he gushed in the happy locker room. "You know when I really knew I could pitch up here? When I had those back-to-back shutouts. I had never thrown two shutouts in a row anywhere."

The consecutive whitewashes were Langston's only shutouts of 1984 but many more seem to be locked up in that solid left arm. A 20-win season is also a definite possibility—especially if Seattle solidifies its bullpen (no Mariner saved more than eight games a year ago). Langston, not known for throwing nine innings, finished what he started only three times in games other than the consecutive shutouts.

Manager Chuck Cottier will take him just the way he is. "We have a nice nucleus with the young kids and the young arms," he says. Cottier knows whereof he talks; Mark Langston is the very heart of that nucleus.

DON MATTINGLY
SUDDENLY LAST SUMMER

CAREER RECORD												
YEAR	CLUB	AVG.	G	AB	R	H	2B	3B	HR	RBI	SB
1979	Oneonta	.349	53	166	20	58	10	2	3	31	2
1980	Greensboro	.358	133	494	92	177	32	5	9	105	8
1981	Nashville	.314	141	547	74	172	35	4	7	98	4
1982	Columbus	.315	130	476	67	150	24	2	10	75	1
	New York, AL	.167	7	12	0	2	0	0	0	1	0
1983	Columbus	.340	43	159	35	54	11	3	8	37	2
	New York, AL	.283	91	279	34	79	15	4	4	32	0
1984	New York, AL	.343	153	603	91	207	44	2	23	110	1

Don Mattingly never hit less than .315 in five minor-league seasons. So it was hardly a surprise when he also hit .300 in his first full year in the majors. But no one expected the one-time Evansville, Indiana, high school pitcher to win the American League batting crown.

"I didn't expect him to be this good this soon," admits Yankee manager Yogi Berra, who had planned to use Mattingly as a part-time outfielder–first baseman before the youngster's hot bat forced his installation as a regular on May 1. "But I knew he was going to be good—and I knew it wasn't going to take long."

On the eve of the 1984 season, it appeared that the Yankees were overloaded with potential first basemen, including Ken Griffey, Roy Smalley, and Don Baylor in addition to Mattingly. But Baylor settled into the designated hitter's job, the other veterans failed to produce, and Mattingly hit whether stationed at first or the outfield.

By All-Star time, he had a .330 average, 12 homers, 53 runs batted in, and a spot on the AL squad (batting once in the July 10 game, as a ninth-inning pinch-hitter against Goose Gossage, he hit a fly ball to left field).

TEAMMATES BATTLE

Three days after the Candlestick Park classic, Mattingly entered into a life-or-death struggle with teammate Dave Winfield, a veteran of 11 seasons, for the batting championship. They occupied the top two spots in the batting race the rest of the season and often exchanged the lead during games over the final month.

Though Winfield had led by 39 points (.371 to .332) on July 12, the veteran's lead was down to two on the eve of the season finale.

Responding to the challenge, Mattingly hit a bloop single to left in the first inning of the game

In his first full big-league season, Don Mattingly was named American League Player of the Year by *The Sporting News*. A consistent lefthanded hitter with a smooth swing, Mattingly edged Yankee teammate Dave Winfield for the batting title in a race that went down to the last day of the season.

against the Tigers, doubled off the right-field wall in the third, doubled down the right-field line in the fourth, flied to center in the fifth, and punched a bad-hop single to right in the eighth.

Winfield hit into a force, walked, stroked an infield single, and lined out. Had Winfield managed a hit in that final at-bat, he would have won the heated race by two-thousandths of a point.

"Getting four hits in that situation shows me some class," said Detroit manager Sparky Anderson after the game. "I'd say Mr. Mattingly is going to be heard from for a long time. That kid is something special.

"I don't think anybody knows how to pitch to him. He doesn't seem to have any holes. He's one of the most impressive young hitters I've seen in a long time. We thought we had good reports on how to pitch him, but we're going to have to start over. Mattingly and Alvin Davis (the Seattle first baseman who took Rookie-of-the-Year honors) are outstanding young players."

PHENOMENAL FIGURES

Like Dave Winfield, Mattingly became a .340 hitter with three five-hit games last summer. The first Yankee batting champion since Mickey Mantle hit .353 in 1956 had impressive numbers at season's end:

- League leader with a .343 average, 207 hit, and 44 doubles
- Ranked second with .537 slugging percentage, trailing Harold Baines
- Ranked fifth with 110 runs batted in
- Finished second among teammates with 23 homers, four less than Don Baylor
- First Yankee to top .340, hit at least 40 doubles and 20 homers, and collect at least 100 RBI in a season since Joe DiMaggio in 1941 (the only other Yankees to reach those levels were Babe Ruth and Lou Gehrig)
- Most hits by a Yankee since Bobby Richardson had 209 in 1962 and most doubles by a Yankee since Red Rolfe had 46 in 1939.

Mattingly, who also hit .401 with runners in scoring position, received two significant post-season awards in recognition of his outstanding season: he was named American League Player-of-the-Year by *The Sporting News* and was voted to the post-season American League All-Star team selected by the players for that publication.

The first baseman's hot finish fueled a Yankee revival that gives New York an air of optimism heading into the 1985 campaign. After finding themselves 17½ games out of first place on June 1—their biggest deficit since World War II—the team went 51-29 over the second half (the best record in baseball) to finish third with an overall mark of 87-75. But Mattingly and his teammates still face the difficult assignment of making up the 17-game margin that separated the Yankees from the front-running Detroit Tigers in the American League East last year.

CONFIDENT STAR

"I always had confidence I could hit .300," insists Mattingly, a three-sport star in high school whose baseball future was clouded by a lack of foot speed (the reason the Yankees waited until the 19th round of the June 1979 amateur draft to select negotiating rights). "I also figured I could drive in a decent number of runs. But I thought I'd hit only 10 or 15 homers.

"It's really a mistake when I hit a home run. It's a great feeling to hit one, but I don't consciously try to do it. Early in the season, I hit a couple in a row and got out of my game. I have to stay within myself."

Playing half his games in Yankee Stadium—a park ideal for lefthanded hitters—helps hike Mattingly's home run total. But batting coach Lou Piniella says the main factor in his success is an understanding of what the pitchers are trying to do, coupled with a willingness to make necessary adjustments.

"For a young hitter, he thinks exceptionally well at the plate," says Piniella, a long-time batting star who retired as a player last year. "By riding his back leg, he generates more power, gets his hands out, and pulls the ball with consistency."

Mattingly went into the 1984 season with a sense of confidence after leading the Puerto Rican Winter League with a .368 average. But a 91-game rookie season with the Yankees also helped—even though a late tailspin at the plate plunged his average from the customary .300 level to .283.

Jax Robertson, now with the Tigers, was the scout who convinced the Yankees to shell out $22,000 to sign Mattingly out of high school—and convince him to postpone college plans—in 1979. Later that year, the Yankees traded Chris Chambliss, their star first baseman, in an effort to plug the catching void left by the death of team captain Thurman Munson. Though Rick Cerone filled the bill for several seasons, the problem had merely relocated—from catcher to first base.

"It was a little frustrating when they kept bringing in veterans," Mattingly admits today. "My attitude was I'd eventually make it to the majors—either with the Yankees or some other team—and I worked at learning to play the outfield because I thought it would speed my progress."

Mattingly was right—but not before the Yankees had tried everyone but Yassir Arafat in a frenzied effort to plug the hole in the infield dike.

The 24-year-old star has already made Yankee fans forget Chambliss and threatens to make the league forget that Eddie Murray, Kent Hrbek, Alvin Davis, and Rod Carew also play first base. A payoff seems imminent; Mattingly earned $80,000—peanuts these days—in 1984.

LARRY McWILLIAMS
BEST LOSER IN BASEBALL

CAREER RECORD										
YEAR	CLUB	W-L	ERA	G	CG	ShO	SV	IP	H	BB	SO
1974	Greenwood	4-3	2.81	11	1	0	0	64	64	23	61
1975	Greenwood	8-4	2.81	17	4	2	0	83	83	19	71
1976	Greenwood	2-2	2.63	8	1	0	0	48	40	13	44
	Savannah	3-8	4.62	16	3	0	1	74	82	33	37
1977	Savannah	8-9	3.36	26	9	3	1	158	153	64	139
1978	Richmond	6-5	2.83	15	7	0	0	108	87	41	78
	Atlanta	9-3	2.82	15	3	1	0	99	84	35	42
1979	Atlanta	3-2	5.59	13	1	0	0	66	69	22	32
1980	Atlanta	9-14	4.94	30	4	1	0	164	188	39	77
1981	Richmond	13-10	4.35	29	8	3	0	178	174	79	157
	Atlanta	2-1	3.08	6	2	1	0	38	31	8	23
1982	Atlanta/Pittsburgh	8-8	3.84	46	2	2	1	159.1	158	44	118
1983	Pittsburgh	15-8	3.25	35	8	4	0	238.0	205	87	199
1984	Pittsburgh	12-11	2.93	34	7	2	1	227.1	226	78	149

As a rookie lefthander with the Atlanta Braves in 1978, Larry McWilliams won nine of 12 decisions in half a season—a strong hint that he had the tools to become one of the best pitchers in the National League.

Though saddled with a sad-sack team, McWilliams also managed to get some national exposure that season: he combined with Gene Garber to stop the 44-game hitting streak of Pete Rose. One reason Rose was stymied was a dazzling grab McWilliams made of a line shot up the middle.

In the post-game news conference, McWilliams appeared in his street clothes; he had showered and dressed while Garber was finishing the game for him.

Rose, upset that the historic streak had ended, saw the pitcher sitting in his chair but failed to recognize the rookie out of uniform.

"Are you going to sit there all night or make room for me?" he demanded.

Atlanta publicist Wayne Minshew, hosting the impromptu media event, turned to Rose and said, "Pete, I'd like you to meet Larry McWilliams."

The veteran infielder, now player-manager of the Cincinnati Reds, has learned all about Larry McWilliams in the six seasons since—but he still yells at him with tongue in cheek.

So do other National League hitters, mostly under their breath. McWilliams sends them back to their dugouts muttering about his combination of forkballs, fastballs, two different curveballs, and even an occasional knuckleball—all delivered with a no-windup motion in rapid-fire succession.

QUICK WORKER

According to Hall of Famer Duke Snider, the one-time Dodger slugger who now broadcasts for the Montreal Expos, "McWilliams is a broadcaster's dream. He pitches as if he's double-parked. All those dips and doodles in his motion distract a hitter. With a pitcher like him, sometimes a hitter finds himself watching the motion, not the ball."

McWilliams learned the style under the tutelage of Johnny Sain, now Atlanta Braves pitching coach, when both men were at Richmond of the International League in 1981.

The pitcher had been returned to the minors by the Braves after the addition of several new pitches to his repertoire had destroyed his pitching rhythm and resulted in poor records over a two-year span. He was so confused that he lost seven of his first eight decisions in Triple-A, prompting lengthy consultations with Sain, a well-known expert at resurrecting lost careers.

"The thing I liked about him," McWilliams recalls, "was that he was as good at listening as he was at teaching. You might ask him something and he'd stop and think, maybe not even give you an answer. A week later, you'd have it worked out yourself."

McWilliams won 12 of his last 15 at Richmond, then two of three late-summer decisions in Atlanta. But he bristled when Braves' manager Joe Torre designated him for relief duty. On June 29, the unhappy pitcher was traded to Pittsburgh for Pascual Perez, then a top-rated minor-league righthander, and shortstop Carlos Rios.

Restored to the role of rotation starter by Chuck Tanner, McWilliams went 6–5 for Pittsburgh in 1982, then had a 15–8 season with 199 strikeouts (most by a Pirate since Bob Veale's 213 in 1969) the following summer.

He was even more effective in '84, when his earned run average dropped from 3.25 to 2.93, but his won-lost record paled in direct proportion to the sudden short-circuiting of Pittsburgh's power production.

At midseason, his 2.52 ERA ranked second to Alejandro Pena of Los Angeles but his record was a disappointing 8–9.

GOOD LOSER

"I guess if you're going to have a losing season, this is the best kind you can have," he said at the time. The pitcher had to be philosophical; twice he lost 1–0, four other times he also lost by a run, and twice he lost by two runs.

"You just wait for the next game and go for it,"

McWilliams has proven to be such a productive pitcher for the Pittsburgh Pirates that the team did not hesitate to use fellow southpaw John Tutor in a winter trade for George Hendrick of the St. Louis Cardinals. McWilliams came to the majors with the Braves before his trade to Pittsburg for righthander Pascual Perez.

he conceded. "You can't live in the past. There will be days when you get runs and don't win. I got seven in Chicago once, but gave up eight."

McWilliams had a rough beginning in 1984; a minor injury cancelled his first start, a home run by Jack Clark ruined his second.

Things turned around by May 12, however, when the 6-5, 175-pound Texan began a streak of 18 consecutive scoreless innings, tops on a Pirate staff that would go on to lead the majors with a 3.11 earned run average.

McWilliams finished strong with an 8–3 mark, one save, and six no-decisions after the All-Star Game. His 2.93 ERA and 227⅓ innings pitched both ranked eighth in the league, but he was succeeded as the All-Star lefthander on *The Sport-*

The fast-working Larry McWilliams was one of several stalwart starters who helped the Pirates compile a 3.11 team earned run average, best in the National League in 1984.

ing News post-season team by San Diego's Mark Thurmond. Nor did he draw as much support in the Cy Young Award voting as he did in 1983, when he finished fifth.

Finishing on the sunny side of .500 for a team that lost 12 more than it won to finish dead last—21½ games off the pace—did provide hope for better things to come.

"It's getting so that people in Pittsburgh recognize me," said McWilliams, who resembles a young version of Jim Kaat on the pitching mound. "Back home in Fort Worth, nobody knows me—except for one guy at Pizza Hut."

RECOGNITION AT LAST

National League batters certainly know who he is; in his 12 victories a year ago, the stingy southpaw posted a microscopic 1.68 earned run average. He was just as devastating at Three Rivers Stadium, where he hurled both of his shutouts and six of his seven complete games to up his career home record as a Pirate to 17–9.

"It seems everything jelled when I got to Pittsburgh," the pitcher suggests. "Chuck Tanner was one reason. He responds to you as an individual and lets you be your own person."

A rugged individualist who likes to hunt and fish in his spare time, McWilliams is always on the lookout to better himself. He developed his devastating forkball quite by accident—while playing catch with a second baseman in Paris (Texas) Junior College.

"He threw a forkball and I thought that might make a great pitch, so I tried it," reveals the pitcher.

McWilliams also believes in helping himself; he's an agile, adept fielder who's smart enough and fast enough to be used as a pinch-runner and talented enough to help himself at bat more than the average pitcher. His hallmark is consistency; he seldom pitches a bad game and is a good bet to last into the late innings before needing relief.

At age 31, he seems to have a bright future ahead—especially if the supporting cast of hitters responds.

JACK MORRIS
PEAKS AND VALLEYS

CAREER RECORD											
YEAR	CLUB	W-L	ERA	G	CG	ShO	SV	IP	H	BB	SO
1976	Montgomery	2-3	6.25	12	0	0	0	36	37	36	18
1977	Evansville	6-7	3.60	20	4	0	0	135	141	42	95
	Detroit	1-1	3.74	7	1	0	0	45.2	38	23	28
1978	Detroit	3-5	4.33	28	0	0	0	106.0	107	49	48
1979	Evansville	2-2	2.38	5	3	0	0	34	22	18	28
	Detroit	17-7	3.28	27	9	1	0	197.2	179	59	113
1980	Detroit	16-15	4.18	36	11	2	0	250.0	252	87	112
1981	Detroit	14-7	3.05	25	15	1	0	198.0	153	78	97
1982	Detroit	17-16	4.06	37	17	3	0	266.1	247	96	135
1983	Detroit	20-13	3.34	37	20	1	0	293.2	257	83	232
1984	Detroit	19-11	3.60	35	9	1	0	240.1	221	87	148

LEAGUE CHAMPIONSHIP SERIES RECORD											
YEAR	CLUB vs. OPP.	W-L	ERA	G	CG	ShO	SV	IP	H	BB	SO
1984	Detroit vs. Kansas City	1-0	1.29	1	0	0	0	7	5	1	4

WORLD SERIES RECORD											
YEAR	CLUB vs. OPP.	W-L	ERA	G	CG	ShO	SV	IP	H	BB	SO
1984	Detroit vs. San Diego	2-0	2.00	2	2	0	0	18	13	3	12

For Jack Morris, the 1984 baseball season had a perfect picture frame. He made his debut with an April 7 no-hitter against the Chicago White Sox, then finished with route-going World Series wins over the San Diego Padres.

Though things were rocky at times in between, the 6-3, 190-pound righthander still led the Detroit Tigers with 19 victories, one below the career peak he established a year before and one less than 1984 league-leader Mike Boddicker of the Baltimore Orioles.

Morris, now in the third year of a four-year, $3.45 million contract, gave manager Sparky An-derson reason to expect more consistency in 1985 because of his strong post-season performance.

He pitched seven strong innings to take an 8–1 victory over the Kansas City Royals in the first game of Detroit's three-game Championship Se-ries sweep, captured a 3–2 triumph in the World Series opener, then topped San Diego again in Game 4, this time by a 4–2 score. Not since Mike Torrez did it for the 1977 New York Yankees had a pitcher completed two games in the same World Series.

He also finished strong during the regular sea-son—3–0 in his last four starts with a 1.39 earned

Jack Morris won 10 of his first 11 decisions in 1984, fueling Detroit's record 35–5 start, then climaxed his season with two complete-game wins in the World Series. Morris has won 103 games over the last six seasons, more than any other American League pitcher.

run average. The native of St. Paul, Minnesota, Detroit's fifth selection in the June 1976 amateur draft, had an even more impressive start.

HEADING FOR 30?

His 4–0 no-hitter, exactly five years after Ken Forsch (then with the Houston Astros) threw the first hitless game in baseball history, sparked Morris to a 10–1 record and 1.79 ERA by Memorial Day. There was talk of a 30-win season—last accomplished by Detroit's Denny McLain in 1968.

"This guy will go in the high 20s this year and has a shot at 30," said Sparky Anderson at the time, "but it will take some luck."

The luck didn't last for Morris. Elbow and shoulder problems surfaced—and so did a volcanic temper that earned the pitcher the nick-

name Mount Morris. He lost six of his next nine, but still secured his second All-Star assignment in seven seasons with a 12–5 record and 3.08 ERA at the break.

Midseason was hardly a happy time, however; plagued by physical and emotional problems, Morris missed several turns, performed poorly in several others, and became the target of criticism from teammates Lance Parrish, Kirk Gibson, Milt Wilcox, and even his mentor, pitching coach Roger Craig.

SPARKY SAYS

In a diary of the season, *Bless You Boys*, Sparky Anderson catalogued some of Morris' problems.

- July 18—"He blamed the umpires for some bad calls and let his temper get the best of him."
- July 19—"Morris resigned as team player representative and also has refused to grant interviews to the press. You can't worry about things like this or it'll drive you nuts."
- August 7—"Jack has got to start pitching some ball games for us. He hasn't given us anything the last four times out."
- September 4—"Morris talked to the press again. I think he's helping himself by breaking the silence. He handled himself well and made me feel real proud."
- October 13—"Everyone keeps asking what happened to Jack in the middle of the season. He's a perfectionist, a winner. He's just got to learn that you can't win every time you go out there."

The teammates said much the same things of the pitcher: Parrish, his catcher, said he was no fun to play with when he got angry, Gibson complained about his pouting, and Wilcox said he put his teammates on edge.

When things are going right for him, Morris is an articulate, affable athlete more than willing to share his time with the media.

SOUNDS OF SILENCE

"I thought by not talking, things would improve," he says in retrospect. "Instead, they only got worse. Everyone was speculating about me and saying outrageous things. I don't want to be considered a bad guy. I feel deep down I'm a good person. People were saying things without asking me first. We're all human, we all have faults, and I didn't like reading about mine."

The first pitcher in Tiger history to lead the team in victories six years in a row, Morris is a power pitcher whose fastball has been timed at 95 miles per hour—certainly among baseball's best, though Dwight Gooden, Nolan Ryan, and Mario Soto, all National Leaguers, may have more consistent quickness.

Morris enjoyed his first 20-win season in 1983 because he coupled a Craig-taught split-fingered fastball (Bruce Sutter's specialty) with the fastball-slider combination, and learned to change speeds off all his pitches. He lost five of his first eight in '83, but later won 10 straight en route to a 20–13 finish. He had 20 complete games and went at least seven innings in 33 of his 37 starts.

"Morris is the best pitcher in either league—and I'm not knocking Steve Carlton," says Cleveland manager Pat Corrales, who once had Carlton in Philadelphia. "He can throw every pitch he has for a strike in any situation."

VICTORY LOG

With 103 wins over the last six years, Morris has more than any American League pitcher and only three less than Carlton. He tied for league leadership with 14 wins in the strike-shortened 1981 season and led the league with 293⅔ innings

pitched and 232 strikeouts two years later. He was the club's first 20-game winner since Joe Coleman in 1973 and the first Detroit strikeout king since Mickey Lolich in 1971.

Shoulder problems slowed his progress in 1977 and 1978—just as they did last year—but Morris has managed to win a minimum of 16 games in every uninterrupted season since. His best game, until the no-hitter, was a one-hit triumph over the Minnesota Twins on August 21, 1980.

The no-hitter was kind of a surprise for the handsome father of two, who turns 30 in May. He walked six—uncharacteristic wildness for a power pitcher who has never walked as many as 100 batters in a season—and issued half of those free passes in the same inning, the fourth.

"I was more nervous in the seventh inning than I was in the ninth," says Morris of the game, which just happened to be the season premiere of NBC's Saturday baseball series. "I knew I had it going in the fifth inning because I usually don't have a no-hitter in the fifth. I looked up at the board and saw the zero. In the eighth, I told Roger Craig I was going to get it."

Morris struck out eight en route to the first Comiskey Park no-hitter since Joel Horlen of the White Sox victimized Detroit on September 10, 1967. Poetic justice, perhaps? For Jack Morris, any well-pitched game is all in a day's work.

DALE MURPHY
GOING FOR MVP AGAIN

YEAR	CLUB	AVG.	G	AB	R	H	2B	3B	HR	RBI	SB
\multicolumn{12}{c}{**CAREER RECORD**}
1974	Kingsport	.254	54	181	28	46	7	0	5	31	0
1975	Greenwood	.228	131	443	48	101	20	1	5	48	5
1976	Savannah	.267	104	352	37	94	13	5	12	55	6
	Richmond	.260	18	50	10	13	1	1	4	8	0
	Atlanta	.262	19	65	3	17	6	0	0	9	0
1977	Richmond	.305	127	466	71	142	33	4	22	90	6
	Atlanta	.316	18	76	5	24	8	1	2	14	0
1978	Atlanta	.226	151	530	66	120	14	3	23	79	11
1979	Atlanta	.276	104	384	53	106	7	2	21	57	6
1980	Atlanta	.281	156	569	98	160	27	2	33	89	9
1981	Atlanta	.247	104	369	43	91	12	1	13	50	14
1982	Atlanta	.281	162	598	113	168	23	2	36	109	23
1983	Atlanta	.302	162	589	131	178	24	4	36	121	30
1984	Atlanta	.290	162	607	94	176	32	8	36	100	19
\multicolumn{12}{c}{**LEAGUE CHAMPIONSHIP SERIES RECORD**}
	CLUB vs. OPP.										
1982	Atlanta at St. Louis	.273	3	11	13	0	0	0	0	0	1

In the long history of the Most Valuable Player Award, established in 1931, no player has won it three years in succession. Nor has any athlete won it more than three times.

At age 29, Dale Murphy has an excellent chance to alter those statements. He's already won two MVP awards—twice as many as home run king Hank Aaron captured in his career—and might have won a third last year if Bob Horner's injury and Chris Chambliss's sudden inability to hit hadn't intervened.

Horner, like Murphy, is capable of hitting .300 and 30-plus home runs but, unlike Murphy, the muscular third baseman is often sidelined by physical problems. While Murphy played all 162 games for the third straight year in 1984, Horner spent all but 32 games out of action with a refracture of the navicular bone in his right wrist.

Without the big bat of Horner behind him in the lineup, Murphy—and Atlanta manager Joe Torre—looked to Chambliss to produce power with the same consistency he had shown in two preceding 20-home run years. The veteran first baseman never got untracked, however, leaving Murphy as the lone power threat in the Braves' lineup. The rival pitchers—no dummies—merely pitched around him.

It's amazing, in retrospect, to realize that the svelte centerfielder still managed a .290 average—second best of his seven-year career—and,

One of the most affable athletes in the game, Dale Murphy is a two-time MVP who excels in all aspects of the game; he's the only active major-leaguer who has hit 30 homers and stolen 30 bases in the same season. Even without a consistent slugger behind him in the braves' batting order last year, Dale Murphy produced his third straight 100-RBI season.

for the third straight year, 36 home runs, tying Mike Schmidt for the league lead. A last-game single knocked in his 100th run, giving Murphy three straight years at the century mark in RBI. He led the majors with a .547 slugging percentage, stole 19 bases, and made only five errors. Study the statistics and it's obvious why a consensus of National League managers suggest Murphy is the league's top star.

POTENTIAL UNLIMITED

"There's no reason that Dale won't be one of the all-time greats in this game," insists Joe Torre, who was replaced by veteran minor-league manager Eddie Haas the day after the '84 season ended.

"He has everything it takes to be a great one," adds Hall of Famer Ralph Kiner, a one-time Pittsburgh slugger who now broadcasts for the Mets.

Aaron, whose 1957 MVP trophy was the last won by a Brave until Murphy took two straight in 1982–83, goes even further in his appraisal.

"He's the most valuable commodity in baseball," says Aaron, currently director of player development for the Braves. "If I were starting a

team and could pick any active player to build around, I'd pick Murphy. He has the potential to do a lot of things in this game no one else has ever done. No one. Not me, not anyone."

Though Murphy, a devout Mormon and family man, is basically a soft-spoken star who seems almost embarrassed by all the attention, the Braves realize his enormous value. The team gave him a five-year contract, valued at $8.1 million, prior to the 1983 campaign. He's been paying them back since.

Even with no long-ball threat hitting behind him in the lineup, the powerful native of Portland, Oregon, finished with a flourish last fall. He hit .327 with seven home runs and 22 RBI in 26 games to win National League Player-of-the-Month honors in September.

Twice, on April 28 at Houston and May 27 against St. Louis, Murphy hit two home runs in a game. But his biggest game of the year did not involve a home run at all; he hammered three doubles and two singles and scored four runs at Busch Memorial Stadium, St. Louis, on August 18.

"There are quite a few things I can do better," Murphy tells stunned listeners. "I have to cut down on strikeouts and stupid errors. I still don't

Once hailed as "the next Johnny Bench," Dale Murphy blossomed into an all-around star only after converting from catcher to first base and, eventually, to the outfield.

have the concentration at the plate I should a lot of times."

CONSISTENCY COUNTS

"The key element to a career is consistency and that is what I want to attain. I've always been a streak player, but now I want to maintain a consistent level of performance."

Don't tell the Houston Astros Murphy isn't consistent; he slammed 10 of his homers against Astro pitching last year, including four against Houston's top lefthanded starter, Bob Knepper. Six of the 10 home runs came during the nine games he played in the Astrodome, widely known as the most difficult home run park in baseball. No visiting player has ever been so productive in the park's 19-year history.

The 6-5, 215-pound slugger was also remarkably productive in 1983, en route to becoming the youngest man to win consecutive MVP citations. He led the league with 121 runs batted in and a .540 slugging percentage, finished second with 36 homers and 131 runs scored, hit for a career-high .302 average, and stole 30 bases to join Aaron as the only Braves ever to reach the 30–30 mark in steals and home runs in the same season (only four other big-leaguers have done it).

"Dale Murphy has an excellent chance to win the Triple Crown," Aaron insists. "I really wanted it when I played but it eluded me. There's no question Dale can lead the league in home runs and runs batted in, and the way he hits the ball to all fields and the way outfielders play him so deep, allowing shallow hits to fall in, he could hit .340 one year. He has baseball instincts you can't teach."

Many baseball insiders say this will be the year that Murphy joins Aaron as the only players to hit at least 40 home runs and steal at least 30 bases in a single season. If he does it, he'll also join Willie Mays and Bobby Bonds as the only players to perform the rare 30–30 feat more than once. Murphy is the only active member of the 30–30 club.

The four-time All-Star, who broke into pro ball in 1974 and reached Atlanta two years later, takes all the possibilities in stride.

HAD HIS DOUBTS

"There was a time I didn't think I'd be able to stay in the minors, much less play in the majors," concedes the former catcher, who once beaned his own pitcher while trying to nail a would-be base-stealer at second base. "I couldn't throw and it was very frustrating. I had all this God-given talent but all of a sudden I couldn't play. I tried to keep it in perspective and not let it affect my relationships with people. Fortunately, I came through."

Though he once caught a one-hitter for Phil Niekro (Cesar Geronimo doubled with one out in the ninth), Murphy was shifted to first base, partially because of the throwing problems and partially to avoid further damage to knees that have twice required surgery. The arrival of Chambliss, acquired from Toronto during the 1979 winter meetings, pushed Murphy to the outfield during spring training of 1980.

"I'm much more relaxed in the outfield," says Murphy. "Maybe the length of the throw compensates for lack of accuracy. If you throw the ball 300 feet and you're off a little bit, the distance compensates. If you throw it 90 feet to second and you're off four or five feet, you're in trouble."

Because he's so good on defense, Pittsburgh pilot Chuck Tanner says of Murphy, "He's one of those few sluggers who helps you even when he's not hitting."

But a better compliment comes from Danny Ozark, who replaced Frank Robinson as Giants' manager last summer: "If you put Murphy and Andre Dawson in the same outfield, you wouldn't need a third outfielder."

What more can anyone say?

EDDIE MURRAY
CONSISTENCY COUNTS

		CAREER RECORD									
YEAR	CLUB	AVG.	G	AB	R	H	2B	3B	HR	RBI	SB
1973	Bluefield	.287	50	188	34	54	6	0	11	32	6
1974	Miami	.289	131	460	64	133	29	7	12	63	4
	Asheville	.286	2	7	1	2	2	0	0	2	0
1975	Asheville	.264	124	436	66	115	13	5	17	68	7
1976	Charlotte	.296	88	299	46	89	15	2	12	46	11
	Rochester	.274	54	168	35	46	6	2	11	40	3
1977	Baltimore	.283	160	611	81	173	29	2	27	88	0
1978	Baltimore	.285	161	610	85	174	32	3	27	95	6
1979	Baltimore	.295	159	606	90	179	30	2	25	99	10
1980	Baltimore	.300	158	621	100	186	36	2	32	116	7
1981	Baltimore	.294	99	378	57	111	21	2	22	78	2
1982	Baltimore	.316	151	550	87	174	30	1	32	110	7
1983	Baltimore	.306	156	582	115	178	30	3	33	111	5
1984	Baltimore	.306	162	588	97	180	26	3	29	110	10

		LEAGUE CHAMPIONSHIP SERIES RECORD									
YEAR	CLUB vs. OPP.	AVG.	G	AB	R	H	2B	3B	HR	RBI	SB
1979	Baltimore vs. California	.417	4	12	3	5	0	0	1	5	0
1983	Baltimore vs. Chicago	.267	4	15	5	4	0	0	1	3	1

		WORLD SERIES RECORD									
YEAR	CLUB vs. OPP.	AVG.	G	AB	R	H	2B	3B	HR	RBI	SB
1979	Baltimore vs. Pittsburgh	.154	7	26	3	4	1	0	1	2	1
1983	Baltimore vs. Philadelphia	.250	5	20	2	5	0	0	2	3	0

Eddie Murray has a fan club in rival dugouts.

Toronto manager Bobby Cox calls him "the best damned hitter there is."

Detroit's Sparky Anderson says, "He's been able to handle success the way success should be handled. God gave him the ability to become a star. He's accepted that and also accepted the responsibility for his team. He knows how good he is but he also knows the responsibility that goes with it."

And Ralph Houk, whose long managerial career ended last fall when he yielded the reigns as Red Sox field boss, notes, "I can't imagine anyone better than Murray with the game on the line. I've watched a lot of hitters go up there against teams I played for or managed and I can't recall anyone who scared me more. When you get Eddie Murray out to win a ballgame, it makes the clubhouse beer taste better."

If consistency counts, no one in baseball beats

A self-made switch-hitter, Eddie Murray is a devastating slugger and smooth fielder who is widely regarded as the best first baseman in the American League.

Murray's numbers. In the last four uninterrupted seasons (a players' strike shaved seven weeks off the 1981 schedule), the switch-hitting first baseman of the Baltimore Orioles has never had less than a .300 batting average, 29 home runs, or 110 runs batted in.

OLDER BUT BETTER

Though he's now in his ninth season at age 29, Murray seems to be getting better with age. Last year, he tied Gary Matthews for the major-league lead in both on-base percentage (.410) and game-winning RBI (19). He led both circuits with 107 walks and was just 13 RBI behind major-league leader Tony Armas. The Murray total was a remarkable achievement for a man who often found the bases cleared by the teammate hitting ahead of him, Cal Ripken, Jr.

"When I came here," reveals Joe Altobelli, now in his third year at the Oriole helm, "everybody told me just to pencil in Eddie for 30 home runs and 100 runs batted in. People take that for granted, but it's just not easy to do that every year."

It was especially difficult in 1984, when designated hitter Ken Singleton's bat went silent, forc-

ing Altobelli to depend on .216 hitter Wayne Gross and rookie Mike Young to supply punch behind Murray. Other clubs reacted by pitching around the 6-2, 200-pound Californian. Murray answered in his usual way—by letting his bat speak for him.

"If I see a ball out over the plate, I'm going to try to hit it," he says. "One of the things that helped my development in the minor leagues was that the Oriole people let me work things out and learn on my own. No one gave me advice when I didn't hit."

SELF-MADE SWITCHER

A natural righthanded hitter who became a self-taught switch-hitter at the end of the Southern League schedule in 1975, Murray is a quick study of enormous talent. Just a year after his first full season of switching, he won American League Rookie-of-the-Year honors. He was an All-Star a year later, and has made the AL squad four times since, but has yet to be named the starter at first base in the controversial fan balloting.

In 1984, Murray had a .315 average, 17 homers, and 72 RBI at All-Star time. But he finished second in the voting to seven-time batting champ

Rod Carew, whose 1984 stats (.292, 3, 26) paled in comparison.

"As long as my teammates know what I'm doing," insists the four-time Gold Glove winner, "and as long as I command respect from opponents, I don't care about publicity. I don't want to deal with the nonsense that goes with notoriety.

"That's why I'm happy with Baltimore. I have good teammates and a team with a tradition of winning. There aren't too many places you can play and be happy."

With Joe Altobelli managing the American League All-Stars, Murray was added to the squad as Carew's understudy and got into the game as a sixth-inning pinch-hitter against Dwight Gooden, baseball's strikeout king last year. Murray doubled—the only hit Gooden surrendered during his two-inning stint.

"Nothing he does surprises me," insists another Oriole All-Star, Cal Ripken. "When Eddie hits, we win—and it's been like that ever since I've been here. I remember him being in a hot streak right after I first came up (in August 1981)."

One of five brothers to play professional baseball, Murray has more than compensated for the failure of the others to reach the major leagues. After the Orioles lost 10 of their first 12 games last spring, the switch-hitting, righty-throwing first baseman turned one-man wrecking crew for a 30-game stretch. His batting average with runners in scoring position during that span was an astronomical .615.

Later in the season, he had a club-record 22-game hitting streak that included a .442 average (34-for-77), five homers, 20 RBI, and 18 walks. Dan Petry and Doug Bair stopped the streak by walking Murray twice—once intentionally—in the game he wore the collar.

GREAT TEAM PLAYER

"One of the best things about Eddie," says Baltimore pitching coach Ray Miller, a long-time observer of the big-league scene, "is that he's never an 'I' man. Some players always talk about themselves but Eddie's just the opposite. Every-thing is 'we' and 'team' and he likes to let his actions speak for themselves. He's uncomfortable doing a interview because he doesn't like to say 'I.' "

Brooks Robinson, who earned a ticket to Cooperstown through his third-base play with the Orioles, agrees with Miller. "He has a good temperament whether he's hot or cold," says Robinson of Murray. "He keeps putting good years together one after the other. He's the man the Orioles look for to carry them through the year. He doesn't miss many games and he's the type who can hit 40 homers in a season—soon."

One reason the Oriole infielder is so successful at bat is his habit of changing his batting stance to get the best view of the pitched ball—a theory previously exploited with considerable success by Rod Carew, Cecil Cooper and, to some degree, Jim Rice.

"If I get one good pitch to hit in each at-bat, that's all I should want," Murray says. "If I don't hit it, I deserve to be out. If you get two good pitches in an at-bat, you're just lucky. Every at-bat is different and I often change from at-bat to at-bat. The changes I make are basically instinctive."

He's homered from both sides of the plate in the same game five times—most recently in 1982—and twice hit three homers in a game.

"It doesn't take much to see why he does these things," Joe Altobelli suggests. "Great hitters have great hands and Murray is one of them."

He's capable of hitting inside fastballs to the opposite field and flicking his bat at the last second to poke a seeing-eye single through the infield. But he's best-known for his three 30-homer seasons—an accomplishment for anyone playing half his games in Memorial Stadium. Only Boog Powell, Frank Robinson, Ken Singleton, Gus Triandos, and Jim Gentile have done it previously for the Birds.

Murray added to his 1984 heroics with nine homers during the Orioles' 14-game post-season tour of Japan. The message for American League pitchers is obvious: Eddie Murray plans to pick up where he left off.

DAN QUISENBERRY
ROYAL RELIEVER

CAREER RECORD											
YEAR	**CLUB**	**W-L**	**ERA**	**G**	**CG**	**ShO**	**SV**	**IP**	**H**	**BB**	**SO**
1975	Waterloo	3-2	2.45	20	1	0	4	44	40	6	41
	Jacksonville	0-1	2.25	6	0	0	1	8	5	4	2
1976	Jacksonville	0-1	2.25	9	0	0	0	12	8	4	6
	Waterloo	2-1	0.64	34	0	0	11	42	28	9	19
1977	Jacksonville	3-1	1.34	33	0	0	6	74	61	11	33
1978	Jacksonville	4-2	2.39	48	0	0	15	64	62	12	29
1979	Omaha	2-1	3.60	26	0	0	5	35	29	10	16
	Kansas City	3-2	3.15	32	0	0	5	40.0	42	7	13
1980	Kansas City	12-7	3.09	75*	0	0	33	128.0	129	27	37
1981	Kansas City	1-4	1.73	40	0	0	18	62.0	59	15	20
1982	Kansas City	9-7	2.57	72	0	0	35*	136.2	126	12	46
1983	Kansas City	5-3	1.94	69*	0	0	45*	139.0	118	11	48
1984	Kansas City	6-3	2.64	72	0	0	44*	129.1	121	12	41

*-Led league

DIVISION SERIES RECORD											
YEAR	**CLUB vs. OPP.**	**W-L**	**ERA**	**G**	**CG**	**ShO**	**SV**	**IP**	**H**	**BB**	**SO**
1981	Kansas City vs. Oakland	0-0	0.00	1	0	0	0	1.0	1	0	0

LEAGUE CHAMPIONSHIP SERIES RECORD											
YEAR	**CLUB vs. OPP.**	**W-L**	**ERA**	**G**	**CG**	**ShO**	**SV**	**IP**	**H**	**BB**	**SO**
1980	Kansas City vs. New york	1-0	0.00	2	0	0	1	4.2	4	2	1
1984	Kansas City vs. Detroit	0-1	3.00	1	0	0	0	3	2	1	1

WORLD SERIES RECORD											
YEAR	**CLUB vs. OPP.**	**W-L**	**ERA**	**G**	**CG**	**ShO**	**SV**	**IP**	**H**	**BB**	**SO**
1980	Kansas City vs. Philadelphia	1.2	5.23	6	0	0	1	10.1	10	3	0

The telephone rings in the bullpen of the Kansas City Royals during the late innings of a close game. Without picking it up, bullpen coach Jim Schaffer knows that the ring of that phone is the cue for The Australian to start warming up.

The Australian is Dan Quisenberry, a 32-year-old righthanded reliever *par excellence* whose unique submarine delivery accounts for his nickname. After all, Quisenberry's assortment of sinkers, sliders, and occasional knuckleballs all come from Down Under.

Those pitches come with such amazing control and consistency that the native Californian has led the American League in saves three straight years (and four of the last five), become the first reliever to save 40-plus games for two years running, and finished second in the Cy Young Award voting in both 1983 and 1984.

"If I didn't win it last year, I don't see how I could expect to win it this year," said Quisenberry last fall, when final results showed fellow reliever Willie Hernandez with 88 points, 17 more than the Kansas City star. So what if Quisenberry saved a record 45 games in 1983 and 44—12 more than Hernandez—in 1984? Nine voting writers had the wisdom to ignore Quisenberry completely when listing the three names on their ballots. As a result, Quisenberry had nine first-place votes, eight seconds, and two thirds.

"Hernandez has been great but he isn't the only guy in the Tiger bullpen," noted former Kansas City manager Jim Frey, who won the club's only pennant in 1980 when Quisenberry saved 33 games and established career peaks in appearances (75) and victories (12). "Look what Quiz has done the last two years. What he did to saves is like what Babe Ruth did to home runs."

Frey could have used Quisenberry during the last three games of the 1984 National League playoffs, when the San Diego Padres scored late against the Chicago Cubs to notch the second rebound from a 2–0 deficit since divisional play began.

SORE SUBJECT

"Did you ever watch the Smurfs on TV?" the pitcher asks. "They have one guy named Grouchy who goes around saying 'I hate this' and 'I hate that.' That's how I feel when somebody asks me about the Cy Young Award."

With a direct hand in 50 of Kansas City's 84 wins in 1984, Quisenberry's value is obvious. The Royals would have hit rock bottom without him—not only last year but over his five full seasons, when he's salvaged more than half his team's victories.

The 6-2, 180-pound pitcher, now in the third year of a $3.2 million four-year contract that contains an option for 1987, doesn't throw the ball by rival hitters but, unlike the fastball relievers who do, his deliveries invariably slice through the corners of the strike zone. Coupling such pinpoint control with the only true submarine

Quisenberry used his unique submarine style to record successive seasons of 45 and 44 saves for the Kansas City Royals.

style in the American League accounts for his success.

"We can play seven-inning games, then bring him in to finish them," says current Kaycee pilot Dick Howser, who was manager of the Yankees when Quisenberry had a win and save in the best-of-five Championship Series between the two clubs in 1980.

"My only worry with Quiz is getting him enough work. He's never told me he couldn't pitch. Even if he's tired, he says he can get two or three batters out. I know he's not going to get out of a jam with a strikeout and the ground ball I want him to get might go through for a hit. But his sinker has the most perfect downward movement of any in the league and I know I can usually depend on him to do the job."

SUPERB CONTROL

Avoiding walks helps. The base on balls—the scourge of relief pitchers—is a potential run a relief pitcher can ill afford in the late innings of a close game. Quisenberry is so reluctant to yield free passes that he makes Jack Benny look like a spendthrift. In the past two seasons, for example, the red-haired reliever has passed just 23 hitters in $268\frac{1}{3}$ innings—by far the best ratio in baseball.

"The key is how few people he walks," says John Wathan, one of Quisenberry's primary

The Rolaids Relief Man Award, given annually to the top bullpenner in each league, has gone to Dan Quisenberry a record four times—including the last three years in a row—since its inception in 1976.

catchers the last few seasons. "He throws strikes and has great movement on the ball—six inches to a foot straight down on every pitch. He constantly comes up with new pitches and the way he delivers them—right out of his uniform—makes it tough for hitters to pick up his pitches."

Jim Rice, long-time slugging star of the Boston Red Sox, agrees: "The man makes great pitches. He's the only one who throws that way and you only see him once or twice in a series. He puts the ball wherever he wants to."

Adds Tiger star Alan Trammell: "It's not tough to put the ball in play against him, it's just tough to hit it where you want to."

Rickey Henderson, yet another admiring rival, recalls, "I didn't know he had a knuckleball until he threw me one with two strikes. I had no chance. I just froze and let it go by. I stared at him

but he just turned his back. I went back to the dugout thinking, 'That's not fair.' "

Quisenberry developed the deceptive pitching style at LaVerne College, where his 194-inning workload as a senior proved so tiring that he began dropping his delivery lower and lower, eventually sinking to a sidearm style. Despite collegiate success, he went undrafted by major league teams and was an amateur free agent when he signed with Kansas City.

HELPFUL ADVICE

He broke into pro ball in 1975 and advanced through the system, reaching the Royals during the summer of 1979 as a one-pitch sidearming reliever. He switched to the submarine style the following spring after extensive tutoring sessions with Kent Tekulve, then the relief ace of the World Champion Pittsburgh Pirates.

"I didn't think I needed to change," recalls Quisenberry, "but Jim Frey told me to copy everything Tekulve did. At first, I felt foreign and off-balance but the coaches said there was better movement on the ball."

Now it is the hitters who feel foreign and off-balance—when they're trying to hit against Quisenberry. He's added a changeup, forkball, rising fastball, slider, and knuckleball to his main staple, the sinkerball, and mixed the pitches so successfully that in 1984 he became the first pitcher to win the Rolaids Relief Man Award three years in a row. Quisenberry and Bruce Sutter, last year's winners, also joined Rollie Fingers as the only four-time winners of the award, created in 1976.

"I have average major league stuff," says the Kansas City savior, "but I do expect perfection out of it. Everyone digs in and gets good swings against me and I expect good hitters to hit the ball hard two out of every three times up. But I've always played for teams whose infielders had good range and I actually expect balls hit off me will go right at somebody."

A clubhouse character whose wife Janie wears a kitchen apron that asks WHERE'S MY RELIEF?, Quisenberry concedes, "Relief pitching is part-time employment. The real heroes are the guys who work two-plus hours every night, not guys like me who work a half-hour or less but just happen to be there when it's time to shake hands."

What Quisenberry accomplishes in his half-hour, however, is what keeps the turnstiles of Royals Stadium spinning—not to mention the heads of rival hitters. Simply stated, he's the best at a difficult craft.

TIM RAINES
OFF TO THE RACES

		CAREER RECORD									
YEAR	CLUB	AVG.	G	AB	R	H	2B	3B	HR	RBI	SB
1977	Sarasota	.280	49	161	28	45	6	2	0	21	29
1978	West Palm Beach	.287	100	359	67	103	10	0	0	23	57
1979	Memphis	.290	145	552	104	160	25	10	5	50	59
	Montreal	.000	6	0	3	0	0	0	0	0	2
1980	Denver	.354	108	429	105	152	23	11	6	64	77
	Montreal	.050	15	20	5	1	0	0	0	0	5
1981	Montreal	.304	88	313	61	95	13	7	5	37	71
1982	Montreal	.277	156	647	90	179	32	8	4	43	78
1983	Montreal	.298	156	615	133	183	32	8	11	71	90
1984	Montreal	.309	160	622	106	192	38	9	8	60	75
	LEAGUE CHAMPIONSHIP SERIES RECORD										
1981	Montreal vs. Los Angeles	.238	5	21	1	5	2	0	0	1	0

Pete Rose, player-manager of the Cincinnati Reds, insists Tim Raines is the best player in the National League.

"Mike Schmidt is a tremendous player and so are Dale Murphy and Andre Dawson," says Rose, who played with Raines in Montreal most of last year, "but Rock can beat you in more ways than any other player in the league.

"He can beat you with his glove, his speed, and his hitting from either side of the plate. As far as running the bases, I don't see how they ever throw him out. But he doesn't do it on speed alone. He knows the pitchers and gets a great jump."

Rose, certain to be enshrined in Cooperstown five years after his playing career ends, has also hung the label "great" on Raines—high praise for a player with only four years of major-league experience.

"He has the perfect disposition for a great player," Rose insists. "He has fun. You can't tell if he's gone 0-for-4 or 4-for-4. I've never seen him in a bad mood."

DRUG PROBLEM

It wasn't always that way for the star left-fielder; in late June 1982, the Expos learned that Raines had a cocaine habit that was obviously interfering with his natural abilities. After spending some $40,000 on that habit in the first nine months of that year, Raines entered the CareUnit Hospital in Orange, California for a month of

Raines has been returned to the leadoff slot by new Montreal manager Buck Rodgers after a brief 1984 trial as the No. 3 hitter. He hit a career-peak .309 last summer.

rehabilitation in October. His wife and parents joined him for the final week.

"I realized how much my career and my family meant to me," recalls Raines, who has eschewed drug use since. "I was in danger of losing both. I learned from the experience. It's a blessing it happened to me when I was so young because it's made me bear down harder since. I hope my play has made a lot of people forget about it."

The fleet Floridian certainly has impressed on the field. While hitting a career-high .309 last summer, he won his fourth straight stolen-base crown and became the first player in baseball history to steal at least 70 bases for four straight seasons. He tied Johnny Ray for league leadership with 38 doubles, finished third with 192 hits, and ranked second with 106 runs scored. He also had a .393 on-base percentage, trailing only Gary Matthews, Tony Gwynn, and Keith Hernandez a year ago.

LOFTY COMPANY

In 1983, when he had 71 runs batted in and 90

stolen bases, Raines became the first player since Ty Cobb of the 1915 Detroit Tigers to have at least 70 steals and ribbies in the same season (Cobb did it twice before 1915, while Clyde Milan and Benny Kauff did it once each).

"Only an unforeseeable injury can keep him from greatness," insists Steve Rogers, long-time star pitcher for the Expos.

Gary Carter, former Raines teammate, agrees: "I see no reason why he can't accumulate 3,000 hits."

Believed by many to have more potential than Joe Morgan, a two-time National League MVP who is now retired, Raines relies on his speed in his approach to all aspects of the game.

A selective hitter who lays off bad pitches, he makes the ideal leadoff man—drawing nearly 100 walks per year, beating out numerous bunts and infield rollers, and slashing line drives up the outfield power alleys. Since he steals almost at will, he is a perennial leader in runs scored (his 133 in 1983 were the most in the National League since 1970); he has been known to score from first on a single or from second on a sacrifice fly or ground ball.

As an outfielder, his speed is also an asset—especially since he is not blessed with a strong throwing arm. A converted second baseman, Raines played center last year to ease the strain on the knees of incumbent centerfielder Andre Dawson, but is returning to left this season while Dawson remains in right.

"I'm sure runners were taking extra bases on me," says Raines, whose close friendship with Dawson helped him through the dark days of 1982. "My arm isn't strong enough for center field. I really don't mind where I play as long as I have the chance to prepare."

It's always possible that new Montreal manager Buck Rodgers will return Raines to second base—a traditional problem spot for the Expos—but the original intent in shifting him was to prevent the wear-and-tear a middle infielder receives. Playing the outfield also reduces the risk of disabling injury—and the Expos can scarcely afford to lose their chief run-producing threat.

A CHANGE IN THE ORDER

Raines was so good at producing runs, in fact, that Bill Virdon, managing the team last year, dropped him to third in the batting order for a spell. When the switch-hitter suffered through a mild slump, he was restored to the more familiar Number 1 spot, on June 11.

"He doesn't go for bad pitches and that's impor-

The fleet leftfielder of the Montreal Expos has stolen 70 or more bases for four straight seasons, a major league record. He is the only player since 1915 to steal at least 70 bases and knock in at least 70 runs in the same season.

tant in batting third," Virdon explained at the time.

Raines had a predictable reaction to the changes: "I know I can hit from either spot and be comfortable. There certainly is a difference, though. I see a lot better pitches, more fastballs, leading off."

The 5-8, 165-pound father of two sons, who signed with the Expos after graduating from his Sanford, Florida high school in 1977, has been a National League All-Star in each of his four seasons. That trend figures to continue, according to baseball insiders.

RISING STAR

"He's improving every day—if that's possible," says an admiring rival, Pittsburgh Pirates' manager Chuck Tanner.

"If anyone ever had million-dollar legs," suggests infielder Chris Speier, a former teammate, "Timmy's got 'em."

Not since Hall of Famer Luis Aparicio did it for the Chicago White Sox in 1956-57-58 had a player led his league in steals each of his first three seasons; in 1981, a season severed by seven weeks because of a player strike, he swiped a

rookie record 71 in just 88 games (Juan Samuel swiped 72 in 160 games last year to break the Raines mark).

"Stealing bases can be as exciting as hitting home runs," Raines says. "The fans come out to the park to see people like Rickey Henderson, Willie Wilson, and me. I like to be in a game that's real close and make things happen. Nobody can be safe all the time, but each time I steal, I feel I will be."

He usually is; Raines now ranks as the top percentage base-stealer in baseball history.

"I rely on good jumps and quickness," he says. "I'm at top speed after one step. You have to have acceleration to be a base-stealer. If you have all of that, it takes a perfect throw."

In 1983, Raines used that speed to put together what mathematician Bill James says was the greatest season ever by a leadoff man; Raines reached scoring position 137 times (32 doubles, eight triples, 11 homers, and 86 steals of second base) and, by scoring 133 runs, set an NL record by accounting for 19.6 percent of the runs the Expos scored that season. He might have been just as effective had he remained in the leadoff slot all last year. The future, for Tim Raines, seems to have no limits.

JIM RICE
INVINCIBLE DESTROYER

		CAREER RECORD									
YEAR	CLUB	AVG.	G	AB	R	H	2B	3B	HR	RBI	SB
1971	Williamsport	.256	60	223	34	57	9	5	5	27	8
1972	Winter Haven	.291	130	491	80	143	20	13	17	87	7
1973	Bristol	.317	119	423	66	134	25	4	27	93	3
	Pawtucket	.378	10	37	7	14	2	0	4	10	0
1974	Pawtucket	.337	117	430	69	145	21	4	25	93	2
	Boston	.269	24	67	6	18	2	1	1	13	0
1975	Boston	.309	144	564	92	174	29	4	22	102	10
1976	Boston	.282	153	581	75	164	25	8	25	85	8
1977	Boston	.320	160	644	104	206	29	15	39	114	5
1978	Boston	.315	163	677	121	213	25	15	46	139	7
1979	Boston	.325	158	619	117	201	39	6	39	130	9
1980	Boston	.294	124	504	81	148	22	6	24	86	8
1981	Boston	.284	108	451	51	128	18	1	17	62	2
1982	Boston	.309	145	573	86	177	24	5	24	97	0
1983	Boston	.305	155	626	90	191	34	1	39	126	0
1984	Boston	.280	159	657	98	184	25	7	28	122	4

Jim Rice considers his 1984 numbers disappointing: a .280 batting average, 28 homers, and 122 runs batted in—17 of them game-winners.

Almost anyone else would have been pleased with such production, but the powerful right-handed hitter from Anderson, South Carolina is used to bigger and better things.

The only man ever to have 35 homers and 200 hits in three straight seasons (1977–79), Rice has had at least 39 homers and 125 RBI three times each in his 11-year career. He's also hit at least .305 in six different seasons, including his Most Valuable Player year of 1978.

Among other things that summer, Jim Rice led the American League with 213 hits, 15 triples, 46 homers, and 139 RBI. His .315 batting average was nothing to sneeze at either.

"The man is just a great hitter," says veteran observer Ralph Houk, his manager with the Boston Red Sox from 1981 through 1984. "Like Mickey Mantle, he hits to all fields with power. As he's matured, he's become more selective, like Al Kaline. I don't know how Jim is going to stack up against other hitters when his career is over, but I do know that if he plays eight or nine more years, you're going to see numbers up there like you've never seen before."

LIKELY TARGET

In eight years, Rice will be 40, a ripe age for baseball retirement, but could be tempted to remain active if he's within shooting range of the 600-home run club. With 304 lifetime homers

Jim Rice has hit 39 home runs in a season three times but won the Most Valuable Player award only after a 46-homer campaign in 1978. He is the only player ever to enjoy three consecutive seasons of 35 homers and 200 hits.

entering the 1985 season, he'll make it by averaging just a shade over 35 homers for the next eight years.

Playing half his games in Boston's Fenway Park would definitely help, but the Red Sox need to come up with compensation commensurate with the abilities of the three-time home run king and six-time All-Star. In January 1979, Rice signed a seven-year pact worth $650,000 per season, a lucrative sum at the time, but he quickly went from the top-paid American Leaguer to the Number 4 earner on his own ballclub.

No less an authority than long-time Red Sox star Ted Williams, whose .344 lifetime batting average paved his path to Cooperstown, says of Rice, "He's a good hitter who needs to be more disciplined. I tell him not to give the pitcher anything. Protect yourself at the plate. Up to ball three, you're going to be swinging at his pitch. Jimmy only walked 44 times last year; he's not waiting."

Rice established a major-league record for grounding into double-plays last year (erasing the 1954 mark of Red Sox slugger Jackie Jensen, who did it 32 times) but still demonstrated an uncanny ability to hit home runs even on tricky pitches. That was also a Ted Williams trait.

The 6-2, 205-pound family man, whose wife and

two children live in suburban Boston in-season and both Anderson and Winter Haven, Florida (the Boston spring training base), otherwise, has fared well in the unenviable assignment of playing left field for the Boston Red Sox.

THE LEFT FIELD LEGACY

Williams started the tradition of excellence when he arrived in 1939, Carl Yastrzemski continued it when he replaced Williams in 1962, and the 1975 arrival of Rice—and his annual defensive improvement—convinced Boston management to shift Yastrzemski to first base in his later years. Yastrzemski's retirement after the 1983 season has made things easier for Rice, according to Williams.

"He might have felt he was Number 2 with Yaz there," suggests Williams, like Yastrzemski a left-handed hitter with tremendous power.

Rice certainly felt like second fiddle to Fred Lynn when both were hot-shot rookie outfielders with the championship Bosox of 1975. Though their stats were comparable, Lynn was clearly superior defensively and was awarded both the Rookie-of-the-Year and Most Valuable Player citations—the only time one man has won both.

"There was no jealousy," Rice says of Lynn, who began a four-year stint with the Angels before the 1981 campaign. "We both wanted what was best for our team."

In 1983, however, Rice abandoned his usual reserve to raise some points about the MVP balloting in which he finished fourth despite leading the league with 39 homers, tying for the lead with 126 RBI, and hitting .305.

"Cal Ripken outhit me by 13 points, but I had 12 more homers and 24 more RBI," said Rice, who also finished behind Eddie Murray and Carlton Fisk. "Is the MVP for the best player or for the best player on a first-place team?"

FIRST-RATE FIGURES

The 1983 Red Sox finished sixth in the seven-team American League East, probably denying Rice a clear shot at an honor he thought he deserved. Several other sour seasons by the Sox have also hurt Rice—with 1979 the prime example. He hit .325 with 39 homers and 130 RBI that summer but Don Baylor (.296, 36, 139) was named MVP after his California Angels won the

Western half of the American League pennant.

His other 39-homer season was 1977, but Rice couldn't have had worse timing; that was the year Rod Carew of the Minnesota Twins hit .388 (with 14 homers and 100 RBI). After his year-long flirtation with .400—last accomplished by Ted Williams in 1941—Carew won the MVP award.

In 1984, Rice was an also-ran in the balloting, ceding the top finish among the Red Sox to home run and RBI king Tony Armas, who ranked seventh.

Armas and Dwight Evans, who shared team MVP honors in voting by the Boston media, teamed with Rice to produce the third 100-RBI outfield in baseball history and spark a second-half Red Sox revival that gives the Fenway faithful hope for this season.

The key to the revival, as usual, was Jim Rice. Saddled with a .217 batting average, three homers, and 21 RBI on May 14, Rice was returned to the customary No. 3 slot in the batting order after opening as the cleanup man.

He homered at Cleveland in his first at-bat from the third slot, then hit .357 with eight homers and 29 RBI over the first 26 games of the batting order switch. He had seven of those RBI in a three-game series at Yankee Stadium, when he had six hits, including a home run, in 11 at-bats.

"When Jimmy starts hitting, we're a much different club," Ralph Houk explained after the Red Sox took 18 of those 26 games. "With Tony Armas hot too, the pitchers can't pitch around him."

Armas, Evans, and Red Sox newcomer Bill Buckner all earned more than Rice last season, but the Red Sox leftfielder was the sole member of the quartet to earn the Big Brother of the Year Award from Boston's Big Brother Association. The honor cited Rice for his exemplary sportsmanship and his contributions to the Big Brother advisory committee in New England.

Two years earlier, he was nominated for an NAACP award for helping to save the life of a 5-year-old child struck by a Dave Stapleton foul ball in the Fenway Park stands. Reacting instantly, Rice jumped into the stands, grabbed the child, and raced through the clubhouse to a waiting ambulance.

One of nine children himself, Rice eschews recognition for such off-the-field heroism, preferring instead to let his diamond endeavors speak for him. "I can't get him out of the lineup," Ralph Houk said last year. Who would want to?

CAL RIPKEN, JR.
SWEET-SWINGING SHORTSTOP

	CAREER RECORD										
YEAR	CLUB	AVG.	G	AB	R	H	2B	3B	HR	RBI	SB
1978	Bluefield	.264	63	239	27	63	7	1	0	24	1
1979	Miami	.303	105	393	51	119	28	1	5	54	4
	Charlotte	.180	17	61	6	11	0	1	3	8	1
1980	Charlotte	.276	144	522	91	144	28	5	25	78	4
1981	Rochester	.288	114	437	74	126	31	4	23	75	0
	Baltimore	.128	23	39	1	5	0	0	0	0	0
1982	Baltimore	.264	160	598	90	158	32	5	28	93	3
1983	Baltimore	.318	162	663	121	211	47	2	27	102	0
1984	Baltimore	.304	162	641	103	195	37	7	27	86	2

	LEAGUE CHAMPIONSHIP SERIES RECORD										
YEAR	CLUB vs. OPP.	AVG.	G	AB	R	H	2B	3B	HR	RBI	SB
1983	Baltimore vs. Chicago	.400	4	15	5	6	2	0	0	1	0

	WORLD SERIES RECORD										
YEAR	CLUB vs. OPP.	AVG.	G	AB	R	H	2B	3B	HR	RBI	SB
1983	Baltimore vs. Philadelphia	.167	5	18	2	3	0	0	0	1	0

Rookie-of-the-Year his first year. MVP his second. What could Cal Ripken do for an encore?

Don't ask the Texas Rangers. On May 6, the All-Star shortstop of the Baltimore Orioles flew out his first time up, then singled, doubled, tripled, and homered in four consecutive at-bats. On July 27, his first game against the Rangers since the May rampage, Ripken tripled in the first, doubled in the third, singled in the fourth, and flew out—just missing a home run—in the sixth. The Rangers wisely walked him in the eighth to avoid the embarrassment of having a player hit for the cycle in consecutive games against the same pitching staff.

Ripken ripped other teams too; his 1984 numbers included a .304 batting average, 27 homers, and 86 runs batted in, boosting his two-year totals to .311 with 54 home runs and 188 RBI—production hardly traditional for a shortstop.

It was in the field where he really impressed, however. For the second straight season, he led the American League in chances and double-plays. He also established a league record with 583 assists and tied the 1969 mark of Leo Cardenas with 880 successful chances (Ripken made 26 errors, pushing his total chances over 900, a mark not reached by any shortstop since Cardenas). Only Ozzie Smith, known as the Wizard of Ozzie

Ripken has capitalized on his enormous promise by winning the Rookie of the Year Award in 1982 and MVP honors a year later. He hits with unusual power for a shortstop; he's hit 27 home runs in each of the past two seasons.

for his exceptional glove work, has topped 900 in recent National League history (1980).

Since 10 of Ripken's errors occurred during a three-week stretch in August, his defensive performance for the bulk of the season seems even more remarkable—especially since some skeptics regard him as a third baseman playing out of position.

WISE MOVE

The 6-5, 210-pound slugger moved to shortstop during his rookie season of 1982. After a month, he had a .123 average as the regular third baseman and was not making Oriole fans forget Brooks Robinson—or even Doug DeCinces.

Then he started to hit—and Earl Weaver, then running the Orioles, realized he could shift the rising star to shortstop without upsetting his rhythm at the plate. The move succeeded—even though the rookie was faced with the challenge of replacing Mark Belanger, as much a defensive legend at shortstop as Robinson was at third.

"If it ever gets to the point where I can't play shortstop, I'll go back to third," says Ripken, who is two inches taller and 25 pounds heavier than he was during his pro ball debut in 1978.

"Sooner or later, I'll settle at a weight that goes with my body, but staying in shape has never been a problem. The weight I've gained since I signed hasn't bothered me. The more you play and the more experience you get, the smarter you become. If I continue to learn all I can about other hitters—and also about our pitchers—then I probably won't have to cover as much ground. I'm going to work on those things, and also try to cut down on my errors—especially throwing so many balls over Eddie Murray's head."

"In modern times, I don't know of two players as valuable to a club as Murray and Ripken," insists Sparky Anderson, manager of the World Champion Tigers. "They're great players who play every inning of every game. Can you imagine what that does for a manager, knowing he can put those two names down in the third and fourth spots on the lineup every day? I can't think of two players who have meant as much to a team. Babe Ruth and Lou Gehrig maybe, but that was before my time."

FORMER PITCHER

Scouted by major-league teams as a pitcher, Ripken might have been a victim of the designated hitter rule (American League pitchers don't bat). Instead, his bat has been pounding American League fences for three seasons.

"Hitting in front of Eddie definitely helps," says Ripken of his slugging teammate. "There are a lot of times when I get better pitches to hit because he's behind me. If I were a pitcher in a jam, I wouldn't want to pitch to him."

Pitchers like the bases to be empty when Murray comes up, but they feel the same way about Ripken, whose 1983 MVP season included league leadership with 211 hits, 47 doubles, and 121 runs scored, plus 27 homers, 102 runs batted in, and a .318 batting average.

There was no inkling of such power production when the rookie Ripken began his professional career; he hit only eight home runs in his first two seasons. As he put on weight and learned pitching patterns, his strength—and his power—materialized. But he says the minor-league apprenticeship was an endless series of adjustments.

"I learned that if I get my hits, the power will come," he says. "I feel fortunate that I've been healthy enough to play every inning for the last two years. My main goal for the future is to play as long as I can and do as much as I can. Nobody knows what his personal best can be until he's played a long time. I wasn't out to win the MVP award in 1983 and I'm not out there to win another one.

"I don't consciously try to hit home runs either; they come with a good swing, good timing, and a little power. I found I can wait on the ball longer and still hit it hard. Young players tend to hurry at the plate, but experience teaches you not to do that."

Ripken constantly puts that experience to the test; just before Labor Day last year, he had a 12-for-22 week (.545) that included two doubles, four homers, 26 total bases, nine RBI, 10 runs scored, five bases on balls, a 1.182 slugging per-

There's always a Ripken on the field for the Orioles; Cal Ripken, Sr., [congratulating his son after a long home run] is Baltimore's third base coach.

centage, and a .630 on-base percentage. The performance earned him American League Player-of-the-Week honors in a unanimous vote.

While the other Orioles collapsed, Ripken and Murray held their own. "In 1983," Joe Altobelli explains, "we had six guys carrying three. In 1984, we had two guys carrying seven."

Ripken is expected to continue sharing the bulk of that burden this summer. His only shortcomings on offense are a lack of speed leaving the batter's box and on the basepaths, a tendency to strike out a bit too often, and a reluctance to be a patient hitter who is willing to accept a base on balls.

"I've become more aware of the strike zone," he says, "And I'm looking harder for my pitch. There's always room for improvement."

Rival pitchers don't want to hear such statements from the two-time All-Star with the $1 million a year contract (through 1987). The Havre de Grace native, who now lives in nearby Aberdeen, Maryland, won't turn 25 until August 24.

"Ripken has the potential to put earth-shattering numbers on the board in the next 10 years," suggests Joe Altobelli.

Baltimore's third base coach echoes those sentiments. And well he should—or his name wouldn't be Cal Ripken, Jr. The father, a catcher-outfielder in the minors from 1957 through 1964, is a long-time organization man who has coached with the parent club since 1976. His proudest moment? The 1983 World Championship generated by his son's MVP season. Both Ripkens believe there's more to come.

RYNE SANDBERG
WRIGLEY FIELD WUNDERKIND

CAREER RECORD

YEAR	CLUB	AVG.	G	AB	R	H	2B	3B	HR	RBI	SB
1978	Helena	.331	56	190	34	59	6	6	1	23	15
1979	Spartanburg	.247	138*	539x	83	133	21	7	4	47	21
1980	Reading	.310	129	490	95	152	21	12	11	79	32
1982	Oklahoma City	.293	133	519	78	152	17	5	9	62	32
	Philadelphia	.167	13	6	2	1	0	0	0	0	0
1982	Chicago, NL	.271	156	635	103	172	33	5	7	54	32
1983	Chicago, NL	.261	158	633	94	165	25	4	8	48	37
1984	Chicago, NL	.314	156	636	114	200	36	19	19	84	32

*—Led league   x—Tied for league lead

LEAGUE CHAMPIONSHIP SERIES RECORD

YEAR	CLUB vs. OPP.	AVG.	G	AB	R	H	RBI	2B	3B	HR	SB
1984	Chicago vs. San Diego	.368	5	19	3	7	2	1	0	0	3

Before the 1984 baseball season, Ryne Sandberg viewed himself as a hit-and-run man, a player whose role as the No. 2 hitter in the Chicago Cubs' lineup was to advance the runner, keep an inning going. He also figured his defensive ability kept him in the lineup.

When Jim Frey arrived as manager last spring, his first task was to convince Sandberg to think differently. Frey, whose batting tips have taken root with such players as George Brett and Darryl Strawberry, obviously succeeded.

"You have the speed and ability to hit 35 to 40 doubles a year, eight to 10 triples, and even some home runs," the manager told the 24-year-old infielder. "You look like you're just trying to meet the ball and I think you can drive it."

Thrice-weekly winter Nautilus work had strengthened the athlete's arms and upper body sufficiently to supply natural power; the only ingredient lacking was the proper mental approach.

"I'm not big on mechanics," Frey says. "Everybody playing is a good natural athlete. The thing that makes one guy outstanding and one guy ordinary is understanding both game and game situations."

By midseason, it was obvious that the manager's message had taken root; Sandberg drew 1,099,824 votes, tops in the league, in the annual All-Star vote of the fans. Twice, he was National League Player-of-the-Week during the first half; once, in June, he was Player-of-the-Month (with a

Originally a shortstop, Ryne Sandberg played a year at third base for the Cubs before blossoming into a Gold Glove second baseman.

.376 average, eight home runs, 21 runs batted in, and six stolen bases). An 18-game hitting streak didn't hurt either.

HISTORIC NUMBERS

By season's end, it became apparent that he had a clear shot at becoming the first player ever to collect 200 hits, 20 doubles, 20 triples, 20 homers, and 20 stolen bases in the same season.

He missed by a whisker (one triple and one home run short), but still managed to lead the league with 114 runs scored, tie for the lead in triples, finish second in hits, tie for second in doubles, and rank third (behind co-home run champions Dale Murphy and Mike Schmidt) with a .520 slugging percentage.

Murphy and Schmidt had won two Most Valuable Player trophies each—and Murphy was going for an unprecedented third straight—when Sandberg surfaced as an overnight sensation, ending the sluggers' four-year monopoly on the coveted citation.

He got 22 of 24 first-place votes to outdistance runners-up Keith Hernandez and Tony Gwynn, who garnered the other first-place ballots.

His best game of the year came on June 23, when the Cardinals took a 7–1 lead over the Cubs in a nationally televised game at Wrigley Field. By the ninth inning, the St. Louis lead had swindled to 9–8 but crack Cardinal reliever Bruce Sutter, en route to a record 45-save season, was on the mound. Sandberg lead off with a home run.

In the top of the 10th, St. Louis scored twice to take an 11-9 lead. Sutter, still on the mound,

walked Bob Dernier with two outs. Sandberg homered again. The Cubs finally won, 12–11 in 12 innings. Sandberg, on the day, had five hits in six at-bats, two home runs, and seven runs batted in.

GOOD TIMING

"That performance came at a time of the season when we were trying to build confidence," Jim Frey remembers. "It was a very big game for us and one of the greatest individual performances I've ever seen in this game."

Sandberg, now in the second year of a lucrative six-year pact with the Cubs, came to Chicago as an extra player in an exchange of shortstops—Ivan DeJesus of the Cubs for Larry Bowa of the Phillies.

At the time of that trade, January 27, 1982, Chicago general manager Dallas Green—former farm chief and field manager of the Phillies—figured on Sandberg as the eventual heir to the aging Bowa at shortstop. He also figured on luring Bob Dernier from the Phils in a subsequent trade.

Sandberg spent his first year with the Cubs at third base, but shifted to second when slugging third baseman Ron Cey arrived from the Dodgers. Blessed with soft hands, plus the ability both to pivot and to start the double-play, Sandberg proved so capable at the new position that the Cubs have abandoned plans of shifting him again—though Bowa will be supplanted at shortstop by young Shawon Dunston in the near future.

Dernier, meanwhile, came to the Cubs (along

centage, 19 game-winning RBI, and 103 walks led the National League, forced pitchers to feed Sandberg a steady diet of fastballs and sliders. With Dernier on his way to a 45-steal season, pitchers didn't want to get too cute with Sandberg and deferred from throwing him the low-and-away curves and changeups that troubled him in the past.

BIG THREE HITTERS

It was no accident that Sandberg, Matthews, and Dernier finished 1-2-3 on the club in runs scored. Nor was it a surprise that Sandberg won his second successive Gold Glove for fielding excellence at second base: he led the league with 550 assists, 870 chances, and a .993 percentage.

"Ryne Sandberg is the best second baseman I've ever played with," says Larry Bowa without hesitation. "That's no rap on Manny Trillo (Bowa's teammate in Philadelphia), but Ryne does everything so effortlessly—goes after and catches almost every ball and has a great arm. Plus he has a great bat. He's simply a natural."

Even in the year of *The Natural*, the veteran's comments were telling.

Sandberg, alone with Julio Franco (now with Cleveland), had been the best infield prospects in the Philadelphia system before both left in swaps that stunned many baseball insiders.

After hearing all the hoopla about his abilities, Sandberg was surprised the Phils let him go—but he was even more surprised by his sudden stardom in Chicago.

"I've gradually improved as a hitter and seem to be putting it all together now," he admitted late last year, "but I'm a little surprised that everything is happening so quickly. I knew I had the ability to do this, but I still have a long way to go both on defense and as a hitter."

Ironically, Sandberg's sensational summer ended on a sour note when the San Diego Padres exploded for a four-run seventh to take a 6–3 victory in the decisive fifth game of the 1984 National League Championship Series. The image that lingers in the minds of the millions who watched it is the bad-hop bullet that Tony Gwynn rocketed past Sandberg for a two-run double, putting the Padres ahead to stay.

It's been 40 years since the Cubs won a pennant—the longest drought in the National League—and one 6-2, 180-pound righthanded hitter is determined to stop that streak. If Ryne Sandberg continues to improve, there's a good chance he'll be able to do it.

In 1984, Ryne Sandberg ended Dale Murphy's two-year hold on the MVP award by leading the Chicago Cubs to their first Eastern Division flag; he narrowly missed becoming the first player ever to notch 200 hits, 20 doubles, 20 triples, 20 homers, and 20 steals in the same season.

with Gary Matthews) in another lopsided deal with the Phillies, on the eve of the 1984 season.

"Hitting behind Bobby has made a big difference," Sandberg suggests. "My first two years in Chicago, we didn't have a true leadoff hitter, a guy who got a lot of walks, had a good on-base percentage, and could steal. He has helped me out and the club even more. It seems like pitchers worried more about him and forgot about me as a hitter."

Matthews, the third-place hitter, also helped; the red-hot leftfielder, whose .410 on-base per-

MIKE SCHMIDT
HOME RUN KING

CAREER RECORD											
YEAR	CLUB	AVG.	G	AB	R	H	2B	3B	HR	RBI	SB
1971	Reading	.211	74	237	27	50	7	1	8	31	3
1972	Eugene	.291	131	436	80	127	23	6	26	91	6
	Philadelphia	.206	13	34	2	7	0	0	1	3	0
1973	Philadelphia	.196	132	367	43	72	11	0	18	52	8
1974	Philadelphia	.282	162	568	108	160	28	7	36	116	23
1975	Philadelphia	.249	158	562	93	140	34	3	38	95	29
1976	Philadelphia	.262	160	584	112	153	31	4	38	107	14
1977	Philadelphia	.274	154	544	114	149	27	11	38	101	15
1978	Philadelphia	.251	145	513	93	129	27	2	21	78	19
1979	Philadelphia	.253	160	541	109	137	25	4	45	114	9
1980	Philadelphia	.286	150	548	104	157	25	8	48	121	12
1981	Philadelphia	.316	102	354	78	112	19	2	31	91	12
1982	Philadelphia	.280	148	514	108	144	26	3	35	87	14
1983	Philadelphia	.255	154	534	104	136	16	4	40	109	7
1984	Philadelphia	.277	151	528	93	146	23	3	36	106	5

DIVISION SERIES RECORD											
YEAR	CLUB vs. OPP.	AVG.	G	AB	R	H	2B	3B	HR	RBI	SB
1981	Montreal vs. Los Angeles	.250	5	16	3	4	1	0	1	2	0

LEAGUE CHAMPIONSHIP SERIES RECORD											
YEAR	CLUB vs. OPP.	AVG.	G	AB	R	H	2B	3B	HR	RBI	SB
1976	Philadelphia vs. Cincinnati	.308	3	13	1	4	2	0	0	2	0
1977	Philadelphia vs. Los Angeles	.063	4	16	2	1	0	0	0	1	0
1978	Philadelphia vs. Los Angeles	.200	4	15	1	3	2	0	0	1	0
1980	Philadelphia vs. Houston	.208	5	24	1	5	1	0	0	1	1
1983	Philadelphia vs. Los Angeles	.467	4	15	5	7	2	0	1	2	0

WORLD SERIES RECORD											
YEAR	CLUB vs. OPP.	AVG.	G	AB	R	H	2B	3B	HR	RBI	SB
1980	Philadelphia vs. Kansas City	.381	6	21	6	8	1	0	2	7	0
1983	Philadelphia vs. Baltimore	.050	5	20	0	1	0	0	0	0	0

Even when he's hurting, Mike Schmidt has always been able to leave the pain in the on-deck circle. The quintessential streak hitter, he is fully capable of carrying a club during one of his hot spells.

From April 30 to May 6, 1984, for example, the veteran third baseman of the Philadelphia Phillies socked home runs in four consecutive games, hit .444 with seven runs scored and seven runs batted in, and was named National League Player-of-the-Week.

Nine days later, batting against Bob Welch in

Schmidt, a notorious streak hitter, is the only active National Leaguer with at least 400 lifetime home runs. The nine-time All-Star has hit at least 30 homers in 10 different seasons and won or tied for National League home run leadership in seven of those ten.

Los Angeles, he became the 20th man (and only active player besides Reggie Jackson) to hit 400 major league home runs.

Only Babe Ruth, Jimmie Foxx, Harmon Killebrew, and Willie McCovey reached 400 in fewer at-bats, but Schmidt refuses to think about the prospects of reaching 500 or 600—both within his grasp if he remains reasonably healthy and consistently productive.

"In my mind, there's no way I'll play more than 15 years," says the Philadelphia star, now in his 13th big-league season. "I'll go to the end of this contract three years from now (1987). A lot will depend on what opportunities I might have. I might want to stay in the game as a broadcaster or manager, but the lifestyle would still be the same: two weeks home, two weeks away. That's difficult on a family."

A personal life has become increasingly important to the nine-time All-Star, whose children will celebrate their fifth and seventh birthdays this year.

"There was a time when being asked to sign an autograph was the biggest thrill in the world for me, but now I'd give anything to walk into a McDonald's with the kids and not be recognized," he says.

HERO OR GOAT?

In Philadelphia, where he has hit at least 30 home runs in 10 different seasons and won or tied

for league leadership in seven of those seasons, Schmidt has instant visibility. He's a hero to legions of admirers—especially impressionable females attracted to his well-groomed red hair, trimmed moustache, and muscular physique— but he's also the focal point of the few but vocal boo-birds who gave the town an unwanted reputation.

"I'll have some negative feelings about Philadelphia when I retire," Schmidt admits. "I think an awful lot about why people boo; I go home nights and think about it. I hear all the time that those things shouldn't bother a veteran player, but we're human beings, and some of us are more sensitive than others.

"I concentrate every second I'm out on that field, trying to do my best for myself, for my kids, for my wife, for my teammates, and for the fans. But how do you convince people of that? How do you convince them that for the two minutes from

Two-time MVP Mike Schmidt tied for home run and RBI leadership last year even though nagging injuries slowed him on the field.

the time I'm on deck until the end of an at-bat, no one is trying harder than I am?"

Plagued early last year with a pulled left thigh muscle, pulled right hip muscle, and sore right knee, Schmidt played anyway—knowing his absence would create a serious void in the Philadelphia batting order.

"Mike is a professional," said Paul Owens, who managed the Phils last year before giving way to John Felske at season's end. "He not only plays hurt but he plays like a man who's fighting to keep his job. Consistency is the only word you can use to describe him."

A look at the record supports that thesis. In 1984, Schmidt tied Gary Carter for RBI leadership with 106—the seventh time he has topped the century mark in runs batted in. His first-inning homer in the nightcap of an end-of-season twin bill with Pittsburgh not only forged the tie with Carter but also created a deadlock for home run leadership with Dale Murphy.

He just missed his eighth season of 100 runs scored and came within four homers of his fourth 40-homer campaign. He hasn't hit less than 31 in any of the last six seasons.

STILL A STANDOUT

Though he'll turn 36 before the end of the baseball season, Schmidt seems at the peak of his game—with the singular exception of his running game. He once stole 29 bases in a season, but doesn't run nearly as much as he used to—concessions to aching knees and advancing age. Managers have also been reluctant to flash him the "steal" sign; why risk injury to the only legitimate long-ball threat in the lineup?

"What I do each day is more important than the statistical levels I reach," the slugger says. "When I'm no longer playing, then I'll reflect on the numbers. I don't want to downplay 400, though. It was a thrill and the response of the 40,000 people in Dodger Stadium is something I'll always remember. But a lot of things have to break right for me to think about 500 or more—my health, my strength, my teammates.

"Besides, I've always been a game-oriented hit-

ter. I'll take a walk early in the game by laying off the high fastball and look toward my next at-bat."

With more than 1,000 career walks, it's obvious Schmidt's power production might have been even more impressive if he hadn't been so selective at the plate—or if he just swung harder.

"I try to just lay the bat on the ball," reveals the powerful Ohio University alumnus. "You don't have to swing hard to hit home runs. Henry Aaron hit more than 700 and you never saw him swing hard."

TOP-DOLLAR SLUGGER

Schmidt, at $2 million per year the highest-paid player in the game, has spent his entire baseball career trying to analyze his hot-and-cold tendencies as a hitter, but he's still stumped for answers.

"One day, I can stand up there when Nolan Ryan is throwing one of his best games ever, take a nice little swing, and throw his best fastball up into the seats. On another night, I'll look for that same swing against Ed Whitson and can't find it. That's mindboggling to me," he concedes.

"In the past few years, I've had stretches of eight or ten bad at-bats, thought about them through and through, made one small adjustment, and hit a three-run homer.

"Nobody in this game goes through six months of positives. What it boils down to is trying to limit the negatives and extend the positives."

Two of the positives for Schmidt last year were his .536 slugging percentage, second in the league to Dale Murphy, and his .383 on-base percentage, fifth in the circuit behind Gary Matthews, Tony Gwynn, Keith Hernandez, and Tim Raines.

The biggest negative—beyond Philadelphia's disappointing .500 season and fourth-place finish—was his atypical defensive play. The eight-time Gold Glove winner made an uncharacteristic 26 miscues, many of them because injuries interfered with previously natural moves.

Mike Schmidt's return to robust health figures to make third base a healthy spot in the Philadelphia lineup once again. That should silence some of the boo-birds—and ease the strain on Schmidt when he does what he does best: batting.

MARIO SOTO
TWIRLER WITH A TEMPER

CAREER RECORD												
YEAR	CLUB	W-L	ERA	G	GS	CG	ShO	SV	IP	H	BB	SO
1975	Eugene	2-3	4.20	5	5	2	0	0	30	33	18	11
1976	Tampa	13-7	1.87	26	25	13	3	0	197	142	80	124
1977	Indianapolis	11-5	3.07	18	18	4	0	0	123	100	61	109
	Cincinnati	2-6	5.31	12	10	2	1	0	61	60	26	44
1978	Indianapolis	9-12	5.01	26	24	6	0	0	160	129	95	121
	Cincinnati	1-0	2.50	5	1	0	0	0	18	13	13	13
1979	Indianapolis	1-1	3.96	15	0	0	0	2	25	20	18	38
	Cincinnati	3-2	5.35	25	0	0	0	0	37	33	30	32
1980	Cincinnati	10-8	3.08	53	12	3	1	4	190	126	84	182
1981	Cincinnati	12-9	3.29	25	25	10	3	0	175	142	61	151
1982	Cincinnati	14-13	2.79	35	34	13	2	0	257.2	202	71	274
1983	Cincinnati	17-13	2.70	34	34	18	3	0	273.2	207	95	242
1984	Cincinnati	18-7	3.53	33		13	0	0	237.1	181	87	185

LEAGUE CHAMPIONSHIP SERIES RECORD											
YEAR	CLUB vs. OPP.	W-L	ERA	G	CG	ShO	SV	IP	H	BB	SO
1979	Cincinnati vs Pittsburgh	0-0	0.00	1	0	0	0	0	2	0	1

Everyone marvels at Mario Soto's fastball, but the changeup is the pitch that made the Cincinnati righthander a National League All-Star three times in five full seasons.

So says Stan Williams, who served as pitching coach for the Reds until Pete Rose replaced Vern Rapp as manager last August.

"Mario has one of the best changeups I've ever seen," insists Williams, a former starter with the Dodgers. "I pitched with Johnny Podres and Carl Erskine, who had great ones, but they threw theirs differently—sort of like they were pulling down the window shade."

Soto throws two changeups—balls which break away from both right and lefthanded hitters—and occasionally mixes in a slider, but the fastball remains the frontispiece of his repertoire.

Without that fastball, the Dominican star could not have accumulated 1,000 strikeouts so quickly. Though he became a full-time starter as recently as the strike-shortened 1981 campaign, he notched the milestone strikeout when he fanned Cubs' pinch-hitter Jay Johnstone on May 17.

"The fastball is still my best pitch," he concedes. "Whenever I'm in trouble, I go to it."

And why not? Soto's fastball has been consistently timed in the mid to upper-90s, with a maximum reading at body temperature: 98.6 miles per hour.

A pair of five-game suspensions short-circuited Mario Soto's bid for his first 20-win season, but he still went 18-7 for a fifth-place ballclub.

By throwing the slider more last year—a suggestion by Williams—Soto won eight of his first nine decisions for a team that struggled to give him adequate offensive backing.

He might have done even better if his temper hadn't intervened.

LOSES HIS COOL

On May 27, in Chicago, and again on June 16, in Atlanta, Soto was the central figure in bench-clearing brawls that produced $6,000 in fines and five-game suspensions from the National League office.

"He has a million-dollar arm and a 10-cent head," says Alex Trevino, a former batterymate who was traded to the Braves last year.

Soto declines to talk about his role in the fights, but Williams offers a paternal perspective.

"He still has to learn self-control, to act like a professional," says the former Cincinnati coach. "It's a lesson I had to learn and Mario and I have sat down and talked about this. What he did had

no malicious intent as far as I could see. He just became frightened more than anything else. Someone was trying to take away his livelihood."

The first suspension didn't hurt the pitcher or his team because a blister on the middle finger of his pitching hand would have forced Soto to miss a start anyhow. The second suspension was a different story, however—and contributed to a dry spell of one month and five days between victories.

Without that long drought, Soto almost certainly would have notched his first 20-victory season—an amazing achievement on a team that lost 22 more games than it won.

Though saddled with anemic support, the 28-year-old flamethrower fashioned an 18-7 log and led the league with 13 complete games. Only Joaquin Andujar of St. Louis won more often in the National League.

En route to his 18 victories, a career high, Soto came within one pitch of his first no-hitter; re-

Soto found success in Cincinnati by combining a flaming fastball with a deceptive changeup.

tired all six batters he faced in the All-Star Game; and became the 17th pitcher in baseball history to register four strikeouts in an inning.

Rival managers noticed.

"If I had to build a pitching staff from scratch, I'd take Soto," said St. Louis pilot Whitey Herzog, mindful that he had both Andujar and record-setting reliever Bruce Sutter on his staff last year.

Pittsburgh's Chuck Tanner agreed: "Soto is as good a righthander as I've seen in baseball. I think he's on his way to being up there with the (Tom) Seavers and the (Don) Drysdales. He has good command of his pitches and is also a good hitter."

SWINGS GOOD BAT

Pitchers like to brag about their hitting, but few have legitimate bragging rights. Soto is an exception. When he got two hits and three runs batted in to beat Houston in the Astrodome September 21, he earned $100 from Cincinnati coach Tommy Helms. Before the season, Helms had bet Soto he wouldn't get more than 14 hits; the Astrodome performance pushed his total two over the mark.

It's not surprising Soto is a capable hitter; he was a catcher—and a good one—as an amateur in the Dominican Republic. Someone got the bright idea to utilize his rifle arm from the pitching mound, and the rest is history. Johnny Sierra discovered him and George Zuraw—though reluctant to part with $1,000 in bonus money—signed him for Cincinnati.

Today, Soto is in the second year of a five-year, $6 million contract that makes him the highest-paid player in Cincinnati history. That's a far cry from the $7.50 for 12 hours' work that Soto earned as a skilled mason in the Dominican Republic.

The pitcher could have earned much more by playing out his option and testing the free agent waters, but said he preferred to stay in Cincinnati.

"I like the city," he said when he signed. "It's quiet, not like New York, and the people have been nice to me."

Off the mound, where he is an intense competitor, Soto is also nice—to media and fans alike.

"There's no one better, left or righthanded," says teammate Dave Parker, who joined the Reds as a free agent before the 1984 campaign. "Some of his episodes on the field might lead you to believe otherwise, but he's a very nice guy and a leader on this team."

COMPARED TO THE GREATS

Soto, flattered by comparisons to Tom Seaver and Don Drysdale, lets his statistics do the talking for him—but there are those who are not content merely to look at the numbers.

When Soto first joined the Reds, in 1977, Sparky Anderson had nothing but minor-league numbers to examine. Anderson, choosing to look at the potential instead, predicted that Soto could be the next coming of Juan Marichal, the star Dominican righthander who is now enshrined in the Baseball Hall of Fame.

It took three years for Soto to harness the changeup that has made him a complete pitcher, but he reached the Rhineland to stay in 1980—and has anchored a somewhat suspect pitching staff since.

Off the field, Mario Soto has also been successful; his wife gave birth to a 7-pound, 3-ounce baby girl in September.

That delightful development helped Soto finish with a flourish; the 6-0, 185-pound righthander pitched a seven-hitter on the final day of the season to beat Houston, 7–6, for his 18th win.

This year, if he stays out of trouble and gets a few more runs in support of his magic on the mound, that elusive 20-game season could finally materialize.

DAVE STIEB
QUALITY ON THE MOUND

		CAREER RECORD									
YEAR	CLUB	W-L	ERA	G	CG	ShO	SV	IP	H	BB	SO
1978	Dunedin	2-0	2.08	4	1	0	0	26	23	1	8
1979	Dunedin	5-0	4.24	8	2	1	0	51	54	28	38
1979	Syracuse	5-2	2.13	7	4	0	0	51	39	14	20
1979	Toronto	8-8	4.33	18	7	1	0	129	139	48	52
1980	Toronto	12-15	3.70	34	14	4	0	243	232	83	108
1981	Toronto	11-10	3.18	25	11	2	0	184	148	61	89
1982	Toronto	17-14	3.25	38	19	5	0	288	271	75	141
1983	Toronto	17-12	3.04	36	14	4	0	278	223	93	187
1984	Toronto	16-18	2.83	35	11	2	0	267	215	88	198

"To me," says Reggie Jackson, "Jim Clancy and Dave Stieb are the same thing as Jack Morris and Dan Petry."

Morris and Petry, the powerful 1-2 pitching punch of the World Champion Detroit Tigers, combined for 37 wins a year ago, so the slugger's comparison was obviously meant to flatter Clancy and Stieb, Toronto's answer to the Tiger tandem.

Though Clancy, at 28, slipped a bit last season, Stieb more than took up the slack. Though he missed most of spring training with a twisted ankle, the 6-1, 190-pound Californian won his first five decisions en route to a 16–8 season—the third straight year he's won at least that many.

His 267 innings pitched led the American League and he ranked second with 198 strikeouts and a 2.83 earned run average. He tied for fourth in starts (35), tied for fifth in winning percentage (.667), tied for ninth in complete games (11) and shutouts (2), and tied for 10th in victories.

ALL-STAR STARTER (AGAIN)

Stieb started the All-Star Game for the second straight year (he hurled three hitless innings to win the 1983 game but lost last year when he yielded two runs in as many innings) and finished eighth—with one third-place vote—in the Cy Young Award balloting.

His best effort was a 6–0 shutout at Kansas City April 28, but he also realized great personal satisfaction from a 2–1 triumph over Minnesota August 26. He fanned 11, a single-game high, against the Twins to launch a streak of 29 strikeouts over 26.1 innings, through September 5. His season strikeout total was both a club mark and a personal peak.

Toronto's Pitcher-of-the-Month in April, June, and July—and co-winner with Clancy in August—Stieb has now won 81 games in six seasons in the majors, all with the Blue Jays. Considering that the team blossomed into a contender only last year, the former All-American outfielder seems to have a reasonable chance to reach 300 victories before he's through.

To get to 300, however, requires a combination of patience, talent, and intestinal fortitude; it takes an average of 15 wins a year for 20 years or an average of 20 wins for 15 years. Fernando Valenzuela, who like Stieb did not play a full major-league season until the current decade began, seems to be the only other young pitcher whose early success stamps him as a future candidate for 300 wins.

Like Fernando, the star lefthander of the Los Angeles Dodgers, Stieb is a reasonably good hitter—though the American League precludes the possibility he can display his prowess at the plate because the designated hitter rule remains in force. That could change by 1986, however, because Peter V. Ueberroth, the new Commissioner of Baseball, says he'll let a summer fan poll decide whether the DH will become universal or extinct (the National League does not use it).

ALL-AMERICAN OUTFIELDER

Stieb actually won All-American honors at Southern Illinois University because of his bat. The collegiate outfielder hit .394 in 1978, the year he turned pro, and was drafted by the Blue Jays only after he pitched two innings of emergency relief on May 3. By coincidence, Toronto player development director Bobby Mattick was in the stands—scouting outfielder Stieb on the recommendation of a Blue Jay bird-dog.

"We hadn't liked him as a hitter—I didn't like his swing," recalls Mattick, who later spent several seasons as Toronto manager.

"But he knocked our eyeballs out as a pitcher. He was absolutely overpowering. He sure as hell opened our eyes when he started pitching."

Before that spring, Stieb had never pitched anywhere—not even in Little League or high school. He was good, but he was so unenthusiastic about abandoning the outfield that Toronto drafted him only in the fifth round of the amateur draft that June; 105 other athletes were selected ahead of him.

He continued dabbling in the outfield, or serving as designated hitter, during his initial season as a pro, at Dunedin of the Florida State League (he went 19 for 99, a .192 average, in 35 games). By 1979, wiser heads prevailed—Dave Stieb became a full-time pitcher. He reached the pitching-poor Blue Jays in time to split 16 decisions that summer.

EXPANDING REPERTOIRE

When he broke in, the handsome righthander had a 92-mile-per-hour fastball and 90-mile-per-hour slider. Eventually, he added a curve and learned to change speeds off his fastball, making him a four-pitch pitcher with the confidence to throw any of them in any situation or any count.

"He comes right at you and has good control," says Rene Lachemann, third base coach of the Boston Red Sox. "He has a tremendously competitive attitude, good stuff, keeps the ball down, and

The durable righthanded ace of the Blue Jays led the American League with 267 innings pitched last year.

fields his position well—all the things a winning pitcher needs to do."

That's why Toronto was quick to secure his signature on a six-year contract that could pay him $1 million per year if he realizes the incentives. One of them, for example, is a $100,000 bonus for winning the Cy Young Award. Another is a $50,000 prize for pitching 275 innings in a season.

The contract ties Stieb to Toronto through 1987 in a marriage that has the potential to be both sweet and stormy. The good news is that Stieb's record is sure to improve in direct proportion to the bullpen help (nonexistent last year) that the Blue Jays give him. The bad news is that Exhibition Stadium, where Stieb pitches half his games, remains one of the most inviting shooting galleries in the majors.

According to analyst Sparky Anderson, manager of the Tigers, "That might be the all-time ballpark. If you hit a ground ball, it's a base-hit. If you hit it in the air, it's out of the ballpark. If I was a hitter here, I'd tell management I'd stay—even for less money."

Until the acquisition of Bill Caudill, who saved 36 games for The Oakland Athletics last summer, the bullpen had been a long-standing Blue Jay problem; no Toronto pitcher saved more than 10 games last year and the best ERA by a Blue Jay reliever was 3.56 (by Roy Lee Jackson).

"The whole team is frustrated," said Stieb in late August after winning once in seven starts. "If the bullpen comes in and loses, or if I stay in and lose, what's the difference?"

It reached a point last year where Bobby Cox, the befuddled Blue Jay field boss, was afraid to lift his ace even when Stieb struggled in the late innings. A tired Stieb, the manager reasoned, was better than any of the fresh arms in his besieged bullpen. Toronto's supposed firemen had become an arson squad, blowing more games than any other relief corps in baseball. A fan banner noted that fact in late summer when it asked general manager Pat Gillick for relief help: C'MON, GILLICK, WE'VE GOT THE FEVER, GET US A RELIEVER.

Stieb, who turned pro in 1978, is tied to Toronto through 1987 by a contract that, with incentives, could pay him $1 million per season.

Dave Stieb was considered for the part—until the Jays realized he was too valuable a commodity as the leading man on the front line. "He knows he can win when he doesn't have good stuff," says catcher Buck Martinez. "When one of his pitches doesn't work, he makes up for it by moving the ball around. That's the mark of a good pitcher."

RICK SUTCLIFFE
BEARING DOWN WITH THE CUBS

CAREER RECORD											
YEAR	CLUB	W-L	ERA	G	CG	ShO	SV	IP	H	BB	SO
1974	Bellingham	10-3	3.32	17	7	2	1	95	79	48	69
1975	Bakersfield	8-16	4.15	28	10	0	0	193	214	68	91
1976	Waterbury	10-11	3.18	30	8	0	0	187	187	45	121
	Los Angeles	0-0	0.00	1	0	0	0	5	2	1	3
1977	Albuquerque	3-10	6.43	17	1	0	0	77	96	63	48
1978	Albuquerque	13-6	4.45	30	6	0	0	184	179	92	99
	Los Angeles	0-0	0.00	2	0	1	0	2	2	1	0
1979	Los Angeles	17-10	3.46	39	5	1	0	242	217	97	117
1980	Los Angeles	3-9	5.56	42	1	1	5	110	122	55	59
1981	Los Angeles	2-2	4.02	14	0	0	0	47	41	20	16
1982	Cleveland	14-8	2.96	34	6	1	1	216	174	98	142
1983	Cleveland	17-11	4.29	36	10	2	0	243.1	251	102	160
1984	Cleveland	4-5	5.15								
	Chicago, NL	16-1	2.69	20	7	3	0	150.1	123	39	155

LEAGUE CHAMPIONSHIP SERIES RECORD											
YEAR	CLUB vs. OPP.	W-L	ERA	G	CG	ShO	SV	IP	H	BB	SO
1984	Chicago vs. San Diego	1-1	3.38	2	0	0	0	13.1	9	8	10

After he won the 1983 Man of the Year Award from the Cleveland chapter of the Baseball Writers Association of America, Rick Sutcliffe was much in demand on the local rubber chicken circuit. Several times, he delighted his audience with this story:

"I dreamed I died and went to heaven. The first thing I saw was (Indians' general manager) Phil Seghi with a really, really ugly woman. I asked why that was and was told, 'Mr. Seghi was bad during his life and because of that he has to spend the rest of his life with her.'

"Then I saw (Indians' president) Gabe Paul with Bo Derek and I said, 'He must have been really,

really good.' But an angel told me I was wrong. 'Bo was really, really bad,' he said."

It was Sutcliffe who was really bad in 1984—bad for Cleveland over the first two months of the season and then bad news for National League hitters the rest of the way.

The season simply got off to a bad start. Saddled with an infected tooth, the 6-7, 215-pound righthander lost 17 pounds in early May, suffered from a loss of equilibrium, and even lost the hearing in his right ear for awhile. These problems precluded his prospects for pitching successfully; his usual pinpoint control evaporated, his repertoire reverted from extraordinary to mediocre, and his competitive fire went the route of the buffalo nickel.

Cleveland, not used to paying $900,000 per year even to superstars, decided Sutcliffe was a burden it did not wish to bear. So it traded him to a team that had a bear for a symbol—the Chicago Cubs. By the time the seven-player waiver swap was completed on June 13, however, Sutcliffe had regained his health—along with his 90-mile-per-hour fastball, hard slider, and several varieties of curves.

A STREAKER IN CHICAGO

He won his first two Cub outings, lost a game to his former Dodger teammates, then took 14 straight (the first time a Cub pitcher has done that since Ed Reulbach in 1909) to pitch the Cubs to their first championship since 1945. Perhaps it was only half a pennant—the title position in the National League East—but the Cubs had not even won that since the advent of divisional play in 1969.

"He's like a guy on a mission," manager Jim Frey said of Sutcliffe last September. "He's out to prove something. He has a 92-mile-an-hour fastball and all the other pitches, but I think the quality everyone talks about is his competitive nature. He wants to do well so badly. A lot of pitchers have good stuff, but he has that extra ingredient."

Sutcliffe, who turns 29 in June, twice ended four-game losing streaks for the Cubs and seven times posted a victory following a Chicago defeat. His 16 wins, coupled with the four at Cleveland, made him the fourth pitcher to win 20 games in a season while pitching for two different clubs. He also became the first pitcher to be traded in the middle of a season in which he won the Cy Young Memorial Award for pitching excellence.

The Chicago righthander was a unanimous selection—the first since Philadelphia's Steve Carlton was the choice of all 24 electors in 1972. The only other unanimous winners in the history of National League Cy Young selections were Sandy Koufax (three times) and Bob Gibson, both members of the Baseball Hall of Fame.

The overwhelming victory was surprising and flattering, since Bruce Sutter saved a record 45 games, Dwight Gooden had a rookie record in strikeouts, and Joaquin Andujar was the loop's lone 20-game winner.

But who could argue with Sutcliffe's 16–1 record, 2.69 ERA, 155 strikeouts in 150⅓ innings pitched, and impressive—for a pitcher—.250 bat-

Sutcliffe seriously considered megabucks contract offers from the Braves, Padres, and the Royals before re-signing with the Chicago Cubs in December.

ting average and six runs batted in? He even homered while pitching a 13–0 victory over the San Diego Padres in the playoff opener—although Cy Young voting stops before post-season play begins.

THREE BAD GAMES

Sutcliffe says he had only three bad games with the Cubs: a 7–1 loss to Los Angeles, a 13–11 win over Cincinnati, and a 6–3 loss in the playoff finale against the Padres.

"He's the kind of pitcher who can win without his good stuff," says Chicago pitching coach Billy Connors. "He has great composure on the mound, is a good fielder, can hold runners, and can hit and bunt."

Sutcliffe has had good seasons before—including a 17-win Dodger season that won him NL Rookie-of-the-Year honors in 1979 and a 17–11 record for the 1983 Indians—but has never had the luxury of a supporting cast that generates so much offense.

Though Rick Sutcliffe was traded to the Chicago Cubs by the Cleveland Indians on June 13, his 16-1 performance the rest of the season convinced Cy Young Award electors to make him the NL's first unanimous selection since Steve Carlton in 1972.

"A lot of guys could have won 16 games the way this team played when I pitched," he said after the season ended. "It sure made pitching easier when they scored six or seven runs a game. If I'd thrown 11 shutouts in a row, I'd be patting myself on the back, but the team deserved a lot of the credit."

Sutcliffe whitewashed the opposition three times after joining the Cubs—June 24 against St. Louis, August 24 against Atlanta, and, in a seven-inning effort coupled with two scoreless relief frames from Warren Brusstar, October 2 against San Diego.

He was especially tough in August, when he

went 6-0 in as many starts, threw two complete games, and fanned 48 batters in 46 innings. His 3.52 ERA for the month helped swell his final figure to 2.69—a mark that is especially impressive for a pitcher who spends half his time in the cozy confines of Wrigley Field.

"I know what that park can do to ERAs," he said, "but earned run average doesn't concern me anymore. I'll take a 10-9 win with the 1-0 wins, just so long as we do win."

ROUTE TO THE MAJORS

The Independence, Missouri native, married and the father of one child, began his professional career at Bellingham, Washington, where the Dodgers sent him following his selection in the first round of the June 1974 amateur free agent draft. He reached the majors to stay in 1979, but suffered from a severe case of the sophomore jinx the next season. Dodger manager Tom Lasorda lost confidence in him, broke a late-season promise to give him a five-inning trial as a long reliever, and a clubhouse tirade resulted. Ignored in post-season play, Sutcliffe was peddled to Cleveland that winter. He refuses to wear the World Series ring he was awarded as a member of that Dodger team.

"I got the check and I got the trophy," he says, "but my pride won't let me wear that ring."

The red-bearded righty figures he has plenty of time to earn a ring, rather than to receive one just for being there. If he keeps pitching over the next few years the way he did in 1984, that wish will probably become a reality.

Just ask the Philadelphia Phillies; they came away shaking their heads after Sutcliffe fanned 15 of them September 3. Only Dwight Gooden, who twice fanned 16 for the New York Mets, and Mike Witt, who registered a single 16-K game for the California Angels, struck out more men in the majors last summer.

"When we got Gary Matthews and Bob Dernier, we became respectable," says Jim Frey of the 1984 campaign. "When we got Rick Sutcliffe, we became winners."

BRUCE SUTTER
THE ULTIMATE FIREMAN

	CAREER RECORD										
YEAR	CLUB	W-L	ERA	G	CG	ShO	SV	IP	H	BB	SO
1972	Bradenton	0-0	0.00	2	0	0	0	5	3	0	4
1973	Quincy	3-3	4.13	40	0	0	5	85	94	27	76
1974	Key West	1-5	1.35	18	0	0	3	40	26	13	50
	Midland	1-2	1.44	8	0	0	0	25	22	6	14
1975	Midland	5-7	2.16	41	0	0	13	67	64	21	50
1976	Wichita	2-1	1.46	7	0	0	1	12	9	4	16
	Chicago, NL	6-3	2.71	52	0	0	10	83	63	26	73
1977	Chicago, NL	7-3	1.35	62	0	0	31	107	69	23	129
1978	Chicago, NL	8-10	3.18	64	0	0	27	99	82	34	106
1979	Chicago, NL	6-6	2.23	62	0	0	37	101	67	32	110
1980	Chicago, NL	5-8	2.65	60	0	0	28	102	90	34	76
1981	St. Louis	3-5	2.63	48	0	0	25	82.1	64	24	57
1982	St. Louis	9-8	2.90	70	0	0	36	102.1	88	34	61
1983	St. Louis	9-10	4.23	60	0	0	21	89.1	90	30	64
1984	St. Louis	5-7	1.54	71	0	0	45*	122.2	109	23	77

*—Led league

	LEAGUE CHAMPIONSHIP SERIES RECORD										
YEAR	CLUB vs. OPP.	W-L	ERA	G	CG	ShO	SV	IP	H	BB	SO
1982	St. Louis vs. Atlanta	1-0	0.00	2	0	0	1	4.1	0	0	1

	WORLD SERIES RECORD										
YEAR	CLUB vs. OPP.	W-L	ERA	G	CG	ShO	SV	IP	H	BB	SO
1982	St. Louis vs. Milwaukee	1-0	5.70	4	0	0	2	7.2	6	3	6

In 1979, Bruce Sutter saved 37 games, tying the National League record shared by Clay Carroll and Rollie Fingers. He split 12 decisions and posted a 2.23 earned run average in 62 outings, and fanned 110 batters in 101 innings.

It was quite a performance for a pitcher whose team had stumbled to a fifth-place finish, losing two more games than it won, and electors for the coveted Cy Young Memorial Award, given annu-ally for pitching excellence, chose him as the National League recipient.

So why didn't Sutter win it last year?

Mike Krukow, a San Francisco starter in 1984, doesn't know. Asked late in the season for his Cy Young choice, Krukow blurted, "Sutter without question. Forty-two saves is just a great achievement. The Cy Young Award goes to the best pitcher in the league, and that's what he's been."

With 45 saves for St. Louis last summer, Bruce Sutter has an excellent chance to join Rollie Fingers as the only relievers to save at least 300 games in a career; he takes a total of 260 saves into the '85 season.

It's ironic that Willie Hernandez, a lefthanded reliever for the Detroit Tigers, took both Cy Young and Most Valuable Player honors in the American League with numbers far inferior to Sutter's.

While Hernandez went 9–3 with 32 saves and a 1.92 earned run mark for the Tigers, Sutter's split-fingered fastball smothered National League hitters. The final numbers were five wins (in 12 decisions), a 1.54 ERA, 63 games finished in 71 appearances, and 45 saves, tying the 1983 major league record of Kansas City submariner Dan Quisenberry.

Maybe Sutter was overlooked because the Cards were also-rans—12½ games from the top of the NL East—while Hernandez was instrumental in a World Championship season. But surely the '84 Cardinals were superior to the '79 Cubs. You figure it out.

"I've been consistent all year," said the 6-2, 190-pound righthander in late summer. "If you do the job 75 to 80 percent of the time, you'll have a good year. I've been more than 75 to 80 percent this year.

"I figure I'm good for 25 to 35 saves every year. If I do that, I figure I've done my job. But to go over 40, you've got to have a lot of luck involved. I got away with some hangers and the guys have made some great plays. Also, the other guys in the bullpen have done a great job ahead of me."

STAR GETS HELP

Sutter also had help last year from long-time mentor Mike Roarke, whose early detection of a delivery flaw enabled the pitcher to overcome his problems of 1983. Roarke, who joined St. Louis as pitching coach before the season opened, had previously worked with Sutter in Chicago (the Cubs sent Sutter to St. Louis in exchange for Ken Reitz, Tye Waller, and Leon Durham on December 9, 1980).

Master and mentor have gone their separate ways again; Sutter opted for free agency, considered offers from seven suitors, and then signed a six-year, $10 million contract with the Atlanta Braves last December 7—giving Cardinal fans new reason to remember the date as a "day of infamy."

The complex contract—worth an estimated $50 million over 36 years when annuities are considered—is a far cry from the $500 the pitcher accepted from the man who signed him off a semi-pro team in 1971: Cub scout Ralph DiLullo.

"I signed with the Braves for three reasons," explains Sutter, who enters his eighth season as the highest-paid pitcher in the game. "One was Ted Turner's willingness to keep building winning ballclubs. Two was the chance to see Dale Murphy play every day. And three was the money—I'd be a fool not to take it."

The fatal flaw for the Cardinals was their failure not to use manager Whitey Herzog in negotiations. That might have changed things, the pitcher concedes.

In Atlanta, Sutter faces three basic changes: a natural-grass infield, a park conducive to home runs, and a pitching coach—Johnny Sain—who has never observed him regularly. Turner, however, anticipates no problems.

"With the addition of Bruce Sutter, we're stronger in pitching than we've ever been before," insists the outspoken owner. "I'm certain he'll be a valuable member of our club for many seasons."

The Sutter signing immediately made the Braves favorites to recapture the National League West title they won in 1982 (the team has since finished second twice). It also made the Cardinals strong candidates to fall out of contention in the NL East. Many memories of Sutter will linger in St. Louis, however.

Among other things, the Cardinals have a World Championship to show for their Sutter years.

In 1982, the bearded father of three had 36 saves and nine wins during the regular season, a win and a save in the three-game playoff sweep of Atlanta, and a win and two saves in the seven-game World Series against Milwaukee. His two innings of hitless relief preserved a 6–3 victory in the finale.

"I definitely wanted to be the one out there pitching and getting that last out," Sutter recalls. "That's what makes a great relief pitcher—confidence in yourself."

Mastery of the split-fingered fastball—a variation of the forkball—gave Sutter the confidence he needed. The pitcher learned the unusual delivery in 1973, when he was a sore-armed Cub farmhand whose career had come to a crossroads. Fred Martin suggested the new pitch and the rest is history.

"It took me a while to master it," says Sutter, who reached the majors three years after he was introduced to the pitch. "I can make eight out of ten of them break and sometimes I might throw 10 or 15 that I can break either way; it depends on the fingers and how I spread them.

"The thumb gives it the overspin. The batter doesn't know which way it will break until it breaks hard."

What's especially amazing about Sutter is that he throws his patented pitch 80 percent of the time, mixing in a fastball just to keep the hitters honest.

HITTERS NOT SURPRISED

"I guess I'm well-advertised," he says. "They know what I'll throw and they're ready for it. I don't think it will surprise anybody when it comes up there."

The only reliever ever to save at least 20 games for eight straight seasons, Sutter is a six-time All-Star who seems headed for eventual enshrinement in Cooperstown. Though no relief pitcher was elected to the Hall of Fame before 1985 (when Hoyt Wilhelm broke the ice), both Sutter and Rollie Fingers—the only man to save 300 games in a career—are logical candidates.

Though just 32 years old, Sutter already ranks second to Fingers with 260 lifetime saves and, with another strong season, could reach 300 this summer.

After learning the split-fingered fastball in the farm system of the Chicago Cubs, Bruce Sutter became an instant success in the major leagues. He was the top target of both Toronto and Atlanta in last fall's free agent market; the Braves won out with a six-year, $10 million pact believed to be worth nearly five times more when annuities are considered.

He's never started in more than 500 big-league outings and doesn't want to try. "I think I'd be nervous as a starting pitcher," says the Mr. Cool of relief pitchers. "Now, I'm completely relaxed for the first five innings of a game. The starters wake up at night and know they're going to start the game. As a relief pitcher, you never have time to get nervous, but you never get the ideal situation either. It's feast or famine."

On September 12, for example, Sutter's first pitch was hit for a game-winning, three-run homer by Philadelphia's Len Matuszek. He also yielded two ninth-inning runs to the Cubs in a vain try for save Number 46 on the last day of the season. "I won't let it ruin my winter," he said. "I had a good year."

That's putting it mildly.

ALAN TRAMMELL
...AND HE HITS TOO!

CAREER RECORD											
YEAR	CLUB	AVG.	G	AB	R	H	2B	3B	HR	RBI	SB
1976	Bristol	.271	41	140	27	38	2	2	0	7	8
	Montgomery	.179	21	56	4	10	0	0	0	2	3
1977	Montgomery	.291	134	454	78	132	9	19	3	50	4
	Detroit	.186	19	43	6	8	0	0	0	0	0
1978	Detroit	.268	139	448	49	120	14	6	2	34	3
1979	Detroit	.276	142	460	68	127	11	4	6	50	17
1980	Detroit	.300	146	560	107	168	21	5	9	65	12
1981	Detroit	.258	105	302	52	101	15	3	2	31	10
1982	Detroit	.258	157	489	66	126	34	3	9	57	19
1983	Detroit	.319	142	505	83	161	31	2	14	66	30
1984	Detroit	.314	139	555	85	174	34	5	14	69	19

LEAGUE CHAMPIONSHIP SERIES RECORD										
YEAR	CLUB vs. OPP.	AVG.	G	AB	R	H	RBI	2B	3B	HR	SB
1984	Detroit vs. Kansas City	.364	3	11	2	4	3	0	1	1	0

WORLD SERIES RECORD										
YEAR	CLUB vs. OPP.	AVG.	G	AB	R	H	RBI	2B	3B	HR	SB
1984	Detroit vs. San Diego	.450	5	20	6	9	6	1	0	2	1

As a general rule, shortstops aren't supposed to hit .300, slug important home runs, or add anything to a team's offense. Most of them bat near the bottom of the batting order, often depart for pinch hitters in late innings, and appear in the lineup only because they hit softly but carry a big glove.

There are three notable exceptions to that rule: American Leaguers Cal Ripken, Jr. of the Baltimore Orioles, Robin Yount of the Milwaukee Brewers, and Alan Trammell of the Detroit Ti-

gers. Yount had the best year of the trio in 1982, Ripken in 1983, and Trammell in 1984.

Though Trammell, unlike Yount and Ripken, was not rewarded with a Most Valuable Player Award, many of his teammates believe he's the best of the talented trio.

"We're fortunate right now in baseball to see three of the greatest shortstops who ever lived," says Darrell Evans, a long-time National League veteran who came to the Tigers as a free agent in 1984. "I think Alan may be the best of all three.

When you see him play every day, you begin to take him for granted, except that he was hitting .360 for a good portion of last season. He's a Gold Glove shortstop who can hit with anybody. He can hit third or fourth in the lineup."

Lance Parrish, the American League's All-Star catcher, echoes Evans's comments: "When we need the big hit, Trammell always seems to come through. Far and away, he leads our club in crucial hits. When you least expect it, Alan hits the ball out of the ballpark."

SERIES SLUGGER

The San Diego Padres learned that lesson in the fourth game of the 1984 World Series. Trammell tagged San Diego starter Eric Show for two-run homers in both the first and third innings, knocking in all the Tiger runs in a 4–2 victory that set the stage for Detroit's World Championship the next day.

Trammell, the first shortstop to homer twice in a World Series game since Rico Petrocelli did it for the 1967 Boston Red Sox, hit .450 (9 for 20) against Padre pitching, scored six runs, and knocked in another six to win the 1985 Pontiac Trans Am given by *Sport* magazine to the World Series MVP.

That followed a .364 performance—including a triple and home run in Game 2—against the Kansas City Royals in the American League Championship Series.

"He's a clone of Pee Wee Reese," says Sparky Anderson, the Tiger manager. "He fields like him, throws like him, behaves like him. He's the best shortstop I've seen—and I had Dave Concepcion at Cincinnati. I love David like a son, but if Alan stays healthy 10 more years, he could be the best shortstop ever. He'll give you 15 home runs a year, hit .300, steal 30 bases, and pick up everything they hit to him."

A June collision with Toronto's Dave Collins produced shoulder problems that kept Trammell from playing shortstop 42 times last summer, but the Tigers had already won 35 of their first 40 (the fastest start in big-league history) en route to a 104-win season.

Despite his aches and pains, Trammell still had the best year of his career, which began with Detroit in 1978. His .314 average ranked fifth in the league and he collected 14 homers, 69 runs batted in, and 19 stolen bases though limited to 139 games. The four-time Gold Glove winner made only 10 miscues at shortstop—the fewest he's made in any uninterrupted season since reaching the majors.

The first shortstop to hit two homers in a World Series game since 1967, Alan Trammell was named 1984 Series MVP by *Sport* magazine. He enjoyed his best year with a .314 average and 14 homers in 1984 but could be even better this summer now that surgery has repaired shoulder and knee problems.

LUCRATIVE PACT

In short, Alan Stuart Trammell justified the signature he put on a seven-year, $2.6 million contract in 1980 (the team has since doubled its value and extended it through 1989).

The two-time All-Star threatens to be even better this season; winter surgery repaired both his right shoulder and left knee—his second knee operation in as many years.

He spent the off-season recuperating at his San Diego home, where an agreeable climate permits outdoor workouts and attention to his golf game—health permitting. Trammell maintains an in-season residence in Redford, a suburb northwest of Detroit, and shares his trilevel home with wife Barbara, a former cheerleader who was his high school sweetheart; three-year-old Lance,

The Gold Glove Award resting on Trammell's trophy shelf is a familiar sight in Detroit; second baseman Lou Whitaker and catcher Lance Parrish also won it.

named for teammate Lance Parrish; and one-year-old Kyle.

"It must have been a thrill for him to play in the World Series and beat the team he grew up watching," Parrish suggests. "Every time he came up in the clutch he came through. He meant so much to us."

San Diego manager Dick Williams, one of Trammell's winter neighbors, wasn't surprised. "We knew what he could do," Williams remembers. "He had an outstanding year. Whenever we threw him a fastball up and over the plate, he conked it."

Trammell, amazed over the fuss at his unexpected offensive contributions, considers himself primarily a defensive player.

"I never thought of myself as a hitter until 1984," he reveals. "And that wasn't until my shoulder injury forced Sparky Anderson to use me as a designated hitter. Even now, I see my job as getting on base for the big guys. I just happened to have a big World Series."

Modesty is another of the positive characteristics of Alan Trammell. The 27-year-old right-handed hitter, a standout high school baseball and basketball star in California, has now had three .300 seasons—including a career-peak .319 in 1983.

TRAMMELL + WHITAKER = SUCCESS

That was the year Trammell and double-play partner Lou Whitaker, the Detroit second baseman, became the first American League keystone

combine to both top .300 since Luke Appling (.301) and Cass Michaels (.308) did it for the 1949 Chicago White Sox.

Though Whitaker, like Trammell, is also a Gold Glove winner, it is the sure-handed shortstop who gets most of the ink.

Darrell Evans explains why: "Watching him every day, I've never seen anyone better at that position. I've seen Ozzie Smith and Johnnie LeMaster in the National League, and they make great plays, but nobody is better fundamentally than Alan. And he's not intimidated at bat like most shortstops. Nobody knocks the bat out of his hands."

Coupled with Parrish, the rifle-armed catcher, and center fielder Chet Lemon, Trammell and Whitaker give Detroit the best up-the-middle defense in the game. Trammell, who has the quickest release of any current shortstop, is at the heart of that dynamic defense. His speed also helps.

In 1983, the 6-0, 175-pound infielder swiped 30 bases, his career high and the most by a Tiger since Ron LeFlore stole 78 four years earlier.

"My job is to get on base," he says. "We'll take it from there. I've learned a lot about the game and I've just tried to be consistent."

The youthful Tiger star is as consistent off the field as he is on.

"Baseball is not the number one thing in my life—my family is," the shortstop insists. "I don't bring the job home with me. We don't talk baseball at home—Barbara's not really a sports fan at all and she doesn't even know whether we win or lose.

"I used to make a lot of appearances, sign autographs, that kind of thing, but I try more and more to shut out the outside world when I'm not at the ballpark. Our success has led to all kinds of increased demands on my time and I have trouble saying no to people."

Trammell is so nice that he even draws accolades from opponents. After becoming the first player to hit a grand slam against Kansas City relief ace Dan Quisenberry, Trammell drew this comment: "I'm happy for him," the pitcher said. "I'm not going to give him another pitch to hit for the rest of his life, but no, I don't hold grudges."

Intimidation wouldn't work anyway; Trammell is simply too sound to succumb. He is to shortstop what Quisenberry is to relieving: the best there is.

FERNANDO VALENZUELA
STILL A KID PITCHER

YEAR	CLUB	W-L	ERA	G	CG	ShO	SV	IP	H	BB
CAREER RECORD										
1978	Guanajuatro	5-6	2.23	16	6	0	1	93	88	46
1979	Yucatan	10-12	2.49	26	12	2	0	181	157	70
	Lodi	1-2	1.13	3	0	0	0	24	21	13
1980	San Antonio	13-9	3.10	27	11	4	0	174	156	70
	Los Angeles	2-0	0.00	10	0	0	1	18	8	5
1981	Los Angeles	13-7	2.48	25	11*	8*	0	192.1*	140	61
1982	Los Angeles	19-13	2.87	37	18	4	0	285	247	83
1983	Los Angeles	15-10	3.75	35	9	4	0	257	245	99
1984	Los Angeles	12-17	3.03	34	12	2	0	261	218	106

*-Led league

YEAR	CLUB vs. OPP.	W-L	ERA	G	CG	ShO	SV	IP	H	BB
DIVISION CHAMPIONSHIP SERIES RECORD										
1981	Los Angeles vs. Houston	1-0	1.06	2	1	0	0	17	10	3

YEAR	CLUB vs. OPP.	W-L	ERA	G	CG	ShO	SV	IP	H	BB
LEAGUE CHAMPIONSHIP SERIES RECORD										
1981	Los Angeles vs. Montreal	1-1	2.40	2	0	0	0	15	10	5
1983	Los Angeles vs. Philadelphia	1-0	1.13	1	0	0	0	8	7	4

YEAR	CLUB vs. OPP.	W-L	ERA	G	CG	ShO	SV	IP	H	BB
WORLD SERIES RECORD										
1981	Los Angeles vs. New York	1-01	4.00	1	1	0	0	9	9	7

After the Watergate scandal engulfed Richard Nixon shortly after his landslide victory over George McGovern in the 1972 presidential election, a bumper crop of bumper stickers began appearing on American highways. Their message: DON'T BLAME ME, I VOTED FOR McGOVERN.

In the wake of the 1984 baseball season, Fernando Valenzuela might be tempted to get a bumper sticker—albeit a Spanish one—for his car. His could say: DON'T BLAME ME, I VOTED FOR RUNS.

The Mexican lefthander, like McGovern in '72

Weight has been a constant concern for the one-time Mexican League standout, who won an unprecedented parlay of rookie and Cy Young honors for the 1981 Dodgers.

and Walter Mondale last November, simply didn't get any support. The workhorse of the Dodger staff appeared in 261 innings, just one-third of an inning less than league leader Joaquin Andujar of St. Louis, tied for second in complete games (12), and ranked second in strikeouts (240). But he finished at 12–17 despite a 3.03 earned run average because he was involved in 13 games in which the Dodgers scored one run or less and a total of 18 in which teammates plated two runs or less.

"Nobody has a chance to win without getting at least one run," said Los Angeles manager Tommy Lasorda in a rare moment of understatement. "Fernando has certainly pitched better than his numbers."

Though Valenzuela walked 106—two shy of the Los Angeles club record set by Stan Williams in 1961—he pitched consistently well after a shaky start. He lost his first two decisions and, after three games, had an embarrassing earned run average that bordered on seven runs per game.

"He can't get his screwball over," said Atlanta manager Joe Torre, trying hard to conceal his delight at the pitcher's predicament. "The more he realizes that he can't get it over and that guys are taking it, the more he'll try to aim it."

FINDING A FLAW

Lasorda and Dodger pitching coach Ron Perranoski, once a prominent Los Angeles lefthander himself, attributed the early problem to an inconsistency in the point at which the pitcher released the ball.

"When Fernando does something wrong, he drops his arms too much," Perranoski explained.

Apparently, the coaching helped. On May 23, Fernando recaptured the magic that made him the only pitcher to win the Cy Young Award and the Rookie-of-the-Year Award in the same season (1981); he fanned 15 Philadelphia Phillies—the league's strikeout high until Dwight Gooden of the New York Mets twice fanned 16 late in the campaign.

By the time the All-Star break approached, Valenzuela had an 8–9 record and respectable 2.97 earned run average. Selected to the National League squad for the fourth straight year, he entered the game as a third-inning reliever for Montreal's Charlie Lea. In the fourth, Fernando fanned Dave Winfield, Reggie Jackson, and George Brett in order. This time, his bumper sticker could have said I STILL GOT IT.

Pitching for the All-Stars is different than pitch-

Though he lost 17 games last season, Valenzuela was largely a victim of non-support; Los Angeles teammates ranked next to last in both offense and defense. The durable lefty has been a National League All-Star four times in as many seasons.

ing for the Dodgers, however. The team's .244 batting average ranked eleventh in the league and represented the worst since the 1970 Dodgers hit .230. Los Angeles also hit bottom with 580 runs scored and ranked next-to-last with 163 errors—a combination of inept offense and defense guaranteed to distort a pitcher's record.

DO-IT-YOURSELF APPROACH

Taking matters into his own hands, Valenzuela threw two shutouts and twice contributed the game-winning run batted in, extending his career mark in that department to six. A former winner of the Silver Bat, given annually to the top hitter at each position, Fernando has shown considerable prowess at the plate during his short big-league tenure. He's appeared as a pinch-hitter and—in a wild 21-inning game with the Cubs on August 18, 1982—actually played right field and left field late in the game.

As a youth playing semipro ball in Mexico, Valenzuela spent most of his time playing first base and the outfield. He pitched only occasionally until age 15, when he signed a professional contract to pitch in the Mexican League. Corito Varona spotted him at Yucatan, recommended Fernando to Dodger scout Mike Brito, and Brito promptly alerted Al Campanis, now general manager in Los Angeles. On July 6, 1979, the Dodgers purchased Fernando's contract.

He learned the screwball from Bobby Castillo in the Arizona Instructional League that fall, pitched at the Double-A level the following summer, and reached the Dodgers to stay that September. He won two decisions in relief, then eight straight as a starter at the outset of the 1981 campaign. Eight of his 13 wins that year were shutouts; five of them came in his first eight starts.

"If he stays healthy, hitters will never catch up with him," said Philadelphia slugger Mike Schmidt, one of many caught up in the wave of Fernandomania that engulfed Los Angeles and electrified its Hispanic population.

"I judge a pitcher by how he gets out of trouble," said Joe Morgan, like Schmidt a two-time National League MVP. "When Fernando is in trouble, he's usually unhittable."

RICH REPERTOIRE

Then, as now, Fernando found success by mixing two screwballs, two fastballs, and a curveball with poise and instincts beyond his years. He won't be 25 until November, but the 5-11, 200-pound lefthander has already drawn praise from the greats of the game.

"We've seen guys show up before who have great stuff," says Sandy Koufax, a great Dodger lefty of the past who is now a member of the Hall of Fame. "This guy has great stuff and can make the pitches when he has to. His control is invaluable.

"I was not the same kind of pitcher Valenzuela is. I didn't have the great change of pace like he does with that one screwball. I changed speeds off my curve.

"If anything, he is more like Juan Marichal. Juan had so many speeds and he had three or four different pitches that he had control of. Barring injury, there is no reason to think Fernando won't join the line of all-time Dodger pitching greats."

Valenzuela's sophomore season seemed to vindicate Koufax's judgment; the portly southpaw posted a 19–13 record and 2.87 ERA, good enough to muster a third-place showing in the Cy Young Award competition that fall. He had another successful season in 1983, when he won 15 of 25 decisions to tie Bob Welch for team leadership in victories.

To some observers, Fernando Valenzuela has compressed a career's accomplishments into four short seasons. Off the field, he has found time to get married, have a child named Fernando Jr., and grace the cover of the November 1984 issue of *L.A. Parent*, as the magazine paid tribute to his "Be Smart: Stay in School" campaign.

It is for his work on the field that he is best known, however. "I feel like a spectator when he pitches," says veteran Dodger infielder Bill Russell. "It's like watching an artist paint a masterpiece."

DAVE WINFIELD
PRODUCING IN PINSTRIPES

CAREER RECORD											
YEAR	CLUB	AVG.	G	AB	R	H	2B	3B	HR	RBI	SB
1973	San Diego	.277	56	141	9	39	4	1	3	12	0
1974	San Diego	.265	145	498	57	132	18	4	20	75	9
1975	San Diego	.267	143	509	74	136	20	2	15	76	23
1976	San Diego	.283	137	492	81	139	26	4	13	69	26
1977	San Diego	.275	157	615	104	169	29	7	25	92	16
1978	San Diego	.308	158	587	88	181	30	5	24	97	21
1979	San Diego	.308	159	597	97	184	27	10	34	118	15
1980	San Diego	.276	162	558	89	154	25	6	20	87	23
1981	New York, AL	.294	105	388	52	114	25	1	13	68	11
1982	New York, AL	.280	140	539	84	151	24	8	37	106	5
1983	New York, AL	.283	152	598	99	169	26	8	32	116	15

DIVISION SERIES RECORD												
YEAR	CLUB vs. OPP.	AVG.	G	AB	R	H	2B	3B	HR	RBI	BB	SO	SB
1981	New York vs. Milwaukee	.350	5	20	2	7	3	0	0	0	1	5	0

LEAGUE CHAMPIONSHIP SERIES RECORD												
YEAR	CLUB vs. OPP.	AVG.	G	AB	R	H	2B	3B	HR	RBI	BB	SO	SB
1981	New York vs. Oakland	.154	3	13	2	2	1	0	0	2	2	2	1

WORLD SERIES RECORD												
YEAR	CLUB vs. OPP.	AVG.	G	AB	R	H	2B	3B	HR	RBI	BB	SO	SB
1981	New York vs. Los Angeles	.045	5	22	0	1	0	0	0	1	5	4	1

Like Bob Horner, Sandy Koufax, and Al Kaline, Dave Winfield is among the few gifted athletes who advanced directly from amateur baseball to the major leagues without stopping at GO, collecting $200, or playing in the minors.

During his senior year at the University of Minnesota, where he was captain of the Gophers baseball team, he had a 13–1 record as a pitcher and a .400 batting average as an outfielder. The first-team All-American selection was the first-round draft pick of the San Diego Padres, who selected fourth in the amateur free agent draft of June 5, 1973.

With nothing to lose, the talent-thin Padres immediately inserted the towering native of St. Paul, Minnesota into their outfield.

He hit only .277 with three homers and 12 runs batted in during his 56-game rookie season, but immediately gave hint of better things to come as a sophomore in 1974. Winfield hit 20 homers, knocked in 75 runs, and displayed the best right-field arm in the National League. Three years later, he received the first of his eight All-Star Game appointments.

The Most Valuable Player of the 1973 College World Series grew tired of playing for an also-ran, however. When the Padres finished fifth, 22 games behind, during Winfield's biggest season (1979), the star righthanded hitter decided to seek greener pastures. That chance came a year later when Winfield played out his option and—after a fierce bidding war involving several clubs—signed a 10-year New York Yankees' contract worth $1,645,704 per season.

HANDSOME DIVIDENDS

Following the strike-interrupted 1981 campaign, his first in New York, Winfield repaid that hefty investment with 30-homer, 100-RBI seasons in 1982 and 1983 and a career-high .340 batting average, second in the American League, in 1984. He and Eddie Murray are the only American Leaguers who have garnered at least 100 RBI in each of the three complete seasons since the strike (Dale Murphy is the lone National Leaguer to do it).

"I try to get better every year," says Winfield, an articulate bachelor who dresses well, drinks little, enjoys Michael Jackson and the company of attractive women, and serves as Yankee player rep. "I haven't had a bad year and that's motivation for me—I don't want to have bad years.

"Hitting is mental. I understand the mechanical or fundamental part; I know what needs to be done and what my body can do. To hit the long ball, I have to pull the ball more. I can hit the ball out of any park but it won't happen with the same frequency if I don't pull."

The 6-6 outfielder, who has played left, center, and right since donning Yankee pinstripes, made a conscious effort to hit for average at the expense of power last season.

"You learn something about yourself every year," he says. "We weren't scoring any runs early in the season (the team was shut out 10 times in its first 38 games) because we weren't getting any men on base. I figured I would try to start something with some base hits and, two months into the season, I had my average up to .330. The home runs and RBI were down so I decided to concentrate on hitting for average. If I had gone the other way, my average would have dropped

Winfield enjoyed three five-hit games in 1984 en route to a .340 batting average, a career high, but teammate Don Mattingly edged him in the batting race. Yogi Berra believes Winfield can become the American League's first .350 hitter since Harvey Kuenn hit .353 for the 1959 Tigers.

and I would have been in the middle of the park somewhere."

Winfield had back-to-back .308 seasons with San Diego but only a .284 career mark going into 1984. So his .377 average on July 5 was quite surprising.

BETTER HITTER

"He's better this way," said batting coach Lou Piniella at the time. "He's using all fields, getting on base, and keeping innings going. Pitchers have changed the way they pitch to him and he's taken advantage of it."

Toronto pitchers learned that lesson on June 3, when Winfield produced the third five-hit game of his career (and first as a Yankee). Not content to rest on his laurels, Winfield had another five-

Dave Winfield was introduced to the New York media by Gene Michael, then Yankee manager, after signing a 10-year contract prior to the 1981 season.

hit game on June 5, against Boston, and still another three weeks later. Only Ty Cobb, in 1922, managed three five-hit games in a more compressed time frame.

In a 26-game span beginning on May 21, Winfield hit .429, scored 21 runs, and drove in 18. From August 17 through September 8, he hit in 20 consecutive games, a career high.

When the smoke cleared in September, Winfield had posted career highs with 106 runs scored, 193 hits, 34 doubles, and his .340 batting average. He lost the batting title by three points only when teammate Don Mattingly, in his first full Yankee season, got four hits (to Winfield's one) in New York's 9–2 win over Detroit in the September 30 season finale. It was the seventeenth time teammates have ranked 1-2 in a league batting race—and the first time since Rod Carew and Lyman Bostock did it for the 1977 Minnesota Twins.

"Winfield has talent, but what makes him different from a lot of guys is that he uses it," says Buddy Bell, the long-time All-Star third baseman of the Texas Rangers. "When he's at the plate, I'm not very comfortable at third base."

Bell is among a host of rivals who wish Winfield had opted for basketball or football instead of baseball; he was drafted by professional teams from all three sports.

Winfield himself sometimes has second thoughts—especially when he locks horns with outspoken Yankee owner George Steinbrenner. Their feuds—over alleged promised payments to the David M. Winfield Foundation, a community relations and youth group organization—have sparked several lawsuits and captured the New York headlines like the second coming of the Billy Martin–Reggie Jackson marriage.

Like Jackson, who spent a year as Winfield's Yankee teammate before signing a free agent contract with the California Angels, Winfield has hardly been a quiet superstar. But he has the statistics to back his boasts.

PEARLS OF WISDOM

"I'm a perfect representative for this club," he says. "I hit, run, and play hard. I speak well. I'm nice to kids, and I appreciate the whole pinstripe tradition. I know I'm outrageous, but I'm in control of my actions and my thoughts. Most people follow, but I can lead—and have fun doing it. I can play."

Yankee manager Yogi Berra, a member of the Baseball Hall of Fame, agrees: "Dave talks a lot, but he does it all, and that's all I care about. He's a good man to have on the team."

Berra is counting on Winfield to become the first righthanded .350 hitter in the American League since Harvey Kuenn hit .353 for the 1959 Tigers (Bill Madlock, at .354 for the 1975 Cubs, was the last NL hitter to do that well). Should the towering outfielder realize that objective, he would have an excellent chance to become the fourth AL batting king in the last 25 years to bat from the right side (righty hitters are at a disadvantage because there are more righthanded pitchers).

"Dave wants people to think of him as a great hitter, a winner," says teammate Don Baylor, a one-time MVP who now serves as designated hitter for New York. "If he didn't care, he'd stick to hitting .280 and go for home runs." Dave Winfield cares.

MIKE WITT
PERFECT PITCHER

		CAREER RECORD									
YEAR	CLUB	W-L	ERA	G	CG	ShO	SV	IP	H	BB	SO
1978	Idaho Falls	7-1	3.56	13	3	0	0	86	88	26	79
1979	Salinas	8-10	5.11	30	2	0	0	141	156	70	94
1980	El Paso	5-5	5.79	12	2	0	0	70	72	39	64
	Salinas	7-3	2.10	13	3	0	0	90	85	35	76
1981	California	8-9	3.28	22	7	1	0	129	123	47	75
1982	California	8-6	3.51	33	5	1	0	179.2	176	47	85
1983	California	7-14	4.91	43	2	0	5	154	173	75	77
1984	California	15-11	3.47	34	9	2	0	246.2	227	84	196

		LEAGUE CHAMPIONSHIP SERIES RECORD									
YEAR	CLUB vs. OPP.	W-L	ERA	G	CG	ShO	SV	IP	H	BB	SO
1982	California vs. Milwaukee	0-0	6.00	1	0	0	0	3	2	2	3

Though Mike Witt first reached the major leagues in 1981, he didn't capitalize on his enormous potential until last year. Much of the credit, the pitcher says, belongs to Harvey Misel.

A relative? A friend? A coach? A fan with a bright idea? Though he is a man of ideas, Misel does not fit any of those categories. Instead, he's a Minneapolis hypnotist with a proven track record in helping baseball players.

Witt consulted with Misel at the suggestion of his California Angels' teammate, Rod Carew, after the veteran first baseman recognized a lack of concentration in the talented pitcher. Misel had helped Carew when the seven-time batting champion played for the Minnesota Twins. As it turned out, Misel also helped Witt.

HYPNOSIS HELPS

"Something he put into my subconscious comes out when I'm on the mound," says the towering righthanded pitcher. "He told me to think that there's no one up at bat and to just throw to the catcher's glove and home plate. I try to get to the point where that's all I really see.

"I knew I had great stuff, the entire league knew I had great stuff. But I hadn't been winning with it."

As soon as Misel's exclusive 1983 contract with the Chicago White Sox expired, Witt made his initial inquiry. The pitcher and therapist had five sessions when California came to Minnesota for a mid-April series and, less than two weeks later, Witt felt a noticeable change.

Hypnosis helped Mike Witt enjoy a 15-win season in 1984 after taking a 23–29 lifetime record into the campaign. With his confidence renewed, the fireballing ace of the Angles threw a season-ending perfect game against the Texas Rangers on September 30.

After overcoming early trouble to pitch an eight-hit, complete-game win over Seattle on May 5, Witt noted, "Last year, I'd know I was struggling and say to myself, 'That's it. I don't have good stuff.' This time, I was determined to stick around until I found my stuff."

The 6-7, 185-pound Californian certainly found his stuff. He led the Angels with 15 wins, 246⅔ innings pitched, and 196 strikeouts (eight behind league-leader Mark Langston of Seattle); ran off a six-game winning streak and 1.76 ERA in mid-season; fanned a league-high 16 batters July 23 against Seattle; and fired a 1–0 perfect game against the Texas Rangers on September 30, the last day of the season.

"I have confidence in my good stuff," he says. "If I throw a good fastball and a guy hits it out, I'll go back to it next time I face him. Before 1984, I

would have been afraid to throw it to him again.

"I would come into games having gotten everybody out twice and say to myself, 'Oh-oh, they've seen everything I have. Next time up, they'll hammer me.'"

LOSING RECORD

That defeatist attitude contributed to the 23–29 career record Witt took into the 1984 season.

According to his catcher, Bob Boone, "He would take no-hitters into the fourth or fifth inning and be in total command, overmatching the hitters, then he'd suddenly lose it without warning. He'd get wild, lose his rhythm, and be gone. The big difference in him was he learned how to maintain a constant rhythm. It's been fun for me to catch him. He's really on top of his game and doing what everyone expected of him all along."

In addition to the sessions with Misel, Witt credits his turnaround to several factors: a successful showing in the Venezuelan Winter League, where he won seven of eight decisions during the 1983–84 campaign; an off-season marriage to former Angel secretary Lisa Fenn; and the addition of Marcel Lachemann as the club's new pitching coach.

That combination apparently struck a chord for Witt, a standard fastball-curveball pitcher who had no confidence in his change-up and considerable control problems before last year. He also had given no indication that he might become a strikeout pitcher.

The 1978 graduate of Servite, California High School had never fanned more than 15 hitters in either schoolboy games or his six-year career in the minors and majors. In fact, his big-league high was eight until he struck out 13 White Sox on June 12.

"I won't forget those 13 strikeouts," he remembers, "but the reaction of the crowd in the Seattle game was different. I knew I was pleasing the home crowd, they were making a lot of noise, and it was a great feeling."

Witt struck out seven of the first eight Mariners and, after striking out the side in the seventh for the second time in the game, had a shot at the major league record of 19 strikeouts in a game (shared by Nolan Ryan, Tom Seaver, and Steve Carlton). But he managed only one strikeout over the last two innings.

Though he didn't get the record, he did get the attention of Seattle manager Del Crandall, a former All-Star catcher. "We can't understand why he isn't 18–0," says Crandall of Witt, who had an 11–7 record at the time.

FINISH WITH A FLOURISH

The Rangers had the same reaction after the season finale. Losing pitcher Charlie Hough, the ace of the Texas staff, said after the game, "It was no contest. I went into the dugout after the third inning and said, 'This guy has a shot at it.' "

Witt fanned 10 and permitted only four balls to be hit to the outfield—including a long drive to right by Larry Parrish leading off the eighth inning. There was one three-ball count—3-and-0 on Wayne Tolleson with one out in the seventh—but Witt threw two straight strikes before retiring Tolleson on a grounder to second. He threw 94 pitches in the one-hour, 49-minute masterpiece.

"I was aware of the no-hitter in the fourth," Witt says, "but at that point I just wanted to win the game. After the seventh, I wanted the whole thing and knew I could do it. I was nervous walking out to the mound in the ninth but only until I threw the first pitch."

In the last inning, Witt fanned Tommy Dunbar, then induced pinch hitters Bobby Jones and Marvis Foley to ground out to second.

"Visibility was zero," said Texas manager Doug Rader of the early autumn sun in Arlington, "but that's no excuse. The kid pitched a helluva game."

The first nine-inning perfect game since Cleveland's Len Barker (now with Atlanta) blanked Toronto, 3–0, on May 15, 1981, Witt's gem was the third no-hitter of the 1984 campaign. Jack Morris of the Detroit Tigers topped Chicago, 4–0, on April 7, and David Palmer of the Montreal Expos pitched a 4–0 perfect game against St. Louis in a contest stopped after five innings by rain on April 21.

It was Witt's first no-hitter since he was a Little Leaguer in Fullerton, California—though he threatened to pull a Bobo Holloman when he hurled seven hitless innings at the Minnesota Twins in his 1981 big-league bow.

"I've never seen anyone as overpowering as Witt," says Preston Gomez, who has coached for both the Angels and Dodgers, "and I've seen Sandy Koufax pitch no-hitters."

The timing, from the pitcher's perspective, was perfect. "Right now it's just a win," he said after the game. "But tomorrow, the day after, and all winter, I can sit ba   and say, 'Hey, I did that.' "

What the Angels would like to know is what Witt plans for an encore.

ROBIN YOUNT
MAIN MAN IN MILWAUKEE

CAREER RECORD											
YEAR	CLUB	AVG.	G	AB	R	H	2B	3B	HR	RBI	SB
1973	Newark	.285	64	242	29	69	15	3	3	25	8
1974	Milwaukee	.250	107	344	48	86	14	5	3	26	7
1975	Milwaukee	.267	147	558	67	149	28	2	8	52	12
1976	Milwaukee	.252	161	638	59	161	19	3	2	54	16
1977	Milwaukee	.288	154	605	66	174	34	4	4	49	16
1978	Milwaukee	.293	127	502	66	147	23	9	9	71	16
1979	Milwaukee	.267	149	577	72	154	26	5	8	51	11
1980	Milwaukee	.293	143	611	121	179	48*	10	23	87	20
1981	Milwaukee	.273	96	377	50	103	15	5	10	49	4
1982	Milwaukee	.331	156	635	129	210*	46	12	29	114	14
1983	Milwaukee	.308	149	578	102	178	42	10	17	80	12

*—Led league

DIVISION SERIES RECORD										
YEAR	CLUB vs. OPP.	AVG.	G	AB	R	H	2B	3B	HR	RBI	SB
1981	Milwaukee vs. New York	.316	5	19	4	6	0	1	0	1	1

LEAGUE CHAMPIONSHIP SERIES RECORD										
YEAR	CLUB vs. OPP.	AVG.	G	AB	R	H	2B	3B	HR	RBI	SB
1982	Milwaukee vs. California	.250	5	16	1	4	0	0	0	0	0

WORLD SERIES RECORD										
YEAR	CLUB vs. OPP.	AVG.	G	AB	R	H	2B	3B	HR	RBI	SB
1982	Milwaukee vs. St. Louis	.414	7	29	6	12	3	0	1	6	0

Robin Yount would like to turn back the clock—with 1982 the logical stopping place. That was the year the strong-armed shortstop led the Milwaukee Brewers to their only American League pennant. The numbers—which earned him near-unanimous selection as Most Valuable Player—included a .331 batting average, 29 home runs, 114 runs batted in, and a league-leading 210 hits, including 46 doubles and 12 triples.

Proving perhaps that offense is contagious, the Brewers slammed 216 home runs, the best team total in the majors, and intimidated all comers until the St. Louis Cardinals, a speed team, literally stole the show in a seven-game World Series showdown.

Most experts expected that trend to continue. Instead, a combination of advancing age and unanticipated ailments plunged Milwaukee to fifth in 1983, 11 games off the pace, and all the way to seventh last year, 36½ games behind.

The chief culprit of the 1984 collapse was a sudden power shortage: the team once known as Harvey's Wallbangers (after manager Harvey Kuenn) was unable to generate even a popgun attack, producing only 96 home runs—the worst output in the 26-team major league network. Manager Rene Lachemann, hailed as one of the game's bright young men on the eve of the season, suffered the same fate as Kuenn the year before: he wasn't invited back.

Robin Yount, however, is a different story. At age 29, the 6-0, 180-pound righthanded hitter is still regarded as the key player on a club that is convinced it won't take much to recapture the glory years. One step in that direction is the return of George Bamberger, who managed Milwaukee to a 95–66 record, best in its history, in 1979.

OUTFIELD FUTURE?

Another step could be the transfer of Robin Yount to center field.

Plagued by back problems in 1983 and frayed tendons in his right shoulder last year, Yount knows a shift to the outfield could prolong his career over the long term and free him to concentrate on his offense over the short term.

"If they feel putting me out there will make the team stronger, I'll go," says Yount, who broke into the majors as Milwaukee's 18-year-old shortstop in 1974. "But I'm not concerned with longevity right now. Last year, I couldn't throw as hard as I normally do, but I could still get the ball to first base in plenty of time."

Off-season surgery corrected the shoulder problem, suggesting Yount could stay at shortstop, but more than 1,500 games at the position have taken a toll physically. Several previous star shortstops have made similar moves in midcareer—notably Hall of Famer Ernie Banks, who was shifted to first base by the Chicago Cubs.

The bad thing about the proposed shift—the brainchild of former Brewers' captain (now special assistant) Sal Bando—is that it would weaken the raging who's-the-best-shortstop debate. Yount was succeeded as American League MVP by Baltimore's Cal Ripken, Jr. and Alan Trammell overshadowed both when he led the Detroit Tigers to the World Championship last year.

Yount's backers point out that he maintained a high level of performance in seasons punctuated by physical ills—his own as well as his team-

An excellent fielder, Yount has been Milwaukee's shortstop since 1974 but shoulder problems—ostensibly corrected by winter surgery—could force his eventual shift to the outfield.

mates'. He hit .308 with 17 homers and 80 RBI in 1983 before slipping to .298 with 16 homers and 80 runs batted in last year. He led the Brewers in all three departments in 1984, the first time since 1976 the team had no .300 hitter and the first time since 1977 no Brewer knocked in 100 runs over a full season. Never in the club's history (dating back to its birth as the expansion Seattle Pilots in 1969) has the team's home run leader hit as few as 16.

ANNOYING AILMENTS

But bear in mind Robin Yount was playing in pain—pain that got so bad he needed a cortisone shot in his right shoulder on June 29. Unable to throw with acceptable velocity, Yount was shifted to designated hitter in an effort to keep his bat in the lineup. Even a Yount in pain is a threat at the plate, the Brewers reasoned.

Despite the aching shoulder, the father of three from Danville, Illinois had several big games in 1984. On May 5, he singled in the tenth inning to score the only run in a 1–0 victory over New York at Yankee Stadium. Little more than a month later, on June 13, he enjoyed a 4-for-4 day that included three doubles as the Brewers took a 6–1 verdict from the Orioles. On July 13, Yount had three hits, including a home run, to collect four

At 29, one-time American League MVP Robin Yount is regarded as the key player in the resurrection of the Milwaukee Brewers.

RBI as Milwaukee edged California, 5–4.

A good two-strike hitter who prefers a steady diet of high fastballs but can also handle breaking balls that are up in the strike zone, Yount bats from a slight crouch and stands deep in the batter's box. Known for down-the-line or in-the-gap extra-base hits, Yount hits to all fields with men on base but sometimes tries to pull the ball for power. Because of that power (he's hit more than 40 doubles three times and more than 20 homers twice), he doesn't bunt much—but he's a good bunter when called upon.

It's doubtful that George Bamberger will flash Yount the bunt sign with any frequency in 1985; the manager needs the three-time All-Star to produce the long ball and doesn't want to take the bat out of his hands.

Bamberger has had success with the Yount psyche before. During spring training of 1978, the unsigned Yount left Milwaukee's Arizona training camp muttering about possible retirement at age 22. Four years of losing teams had gotten to him.

"It wasn't much fun in those days," Yount remembers. "You have a choice of things in life and if you're not enjoying them, you look for other things."

QUIET PERSUASION

Bamberger and general manager Harry Dalton—the men who would transform the Brewers from also-rans to league champions—had just arrived when Yount pulled his walkout. Bamberger used his fatherly guiles to persuade his petulant star to return—several weeks after the season had started. With Yount a key contributer, the club finished a surprising third. Two years later, the shortstop was an All-Star; four years later, he was the fans' choice to start the All-Star Game, the leader of a championship club, and an MVP. He was also the first American League shortstop to lead the league in slugging and total bases and the first to hit .300 with at least 20 homers and 100 RBI. After the season, he was voted the Gold Glove for fielding excellence at his position.

Yount, the Brewers' first choice in the June 1973 draft of amateur free agents, played only 64 minor-league games—at Newark of the Class A New York–Penn League—before reaching Milwaukee. He impressed manager Del Crandall so much during the spring of 1974 that Robin Yount found himself a major-league regular less than a year after he graduated from Taft High School in Woodland Hills, California.

Today, the Scottsdale, Arizona resident spends his off-the-diamond hours golfing, fishing, riding motorcycles, and enjoying a family that includes older brothers Joe and Larry, plus wife Michele and parents Phil and Marion. Larry, a one-time pitcher in the Houston Astros' organization who now serves as Robin's agent, exposed the kid shortstop to pro ball, whetting the appetite of the future Milwaukee star for a career of his own.

"He worked out with my teams," says Larry. "He was pretty good for a young guy." At 29, Robin Yount is more than pretty good—he's one of the best.

1984 LEAGUE STANDINGS

1984 NATIONAL LEAGUE STANDINGS

WESTERN DIVISION	W	L	Pct.	GB	EASTERN DIVISION	W	L	Pct.	GB
San Diego	92	70	.568	—	Chicago	96	65	.596	—
Atlanta	80	82	.494	12	New York	90	72	.556	6.5
Houston	80	82	.494	12	St. Louis	84	78	.519	12.5
Los Angeles	79	83	.488	13	Philadelphia	81	81	.500	15.5
Cincinnati	70	92	.432	22	Montreal	78	83	.484	18
San Francisco	66	96	.407	26	Pittsburgh	75	87	.463	21.5

1984 AMERICAN LEAGUE STANDINGS

WESTERN DIVISION	W	L	Pct.	GB	EASTERN DIVISION	W	L	Pct.	GB
Kansas City	84	78	.519	—	Detroit	104	58	.642	—
California	81	81	.500	3	Toronto	89	73	.549	15
Minnesota	81	81	.500	3	New York	87	75	.537	17
Oakland	77	85	.500	7	Boston	86	76	.531	18
Chicago	74	88	.475	10	Baltimore	85	77	.525	19
Seattle	74	88	.457	10	Cleveland	75	87	.463	29
Texas	69	92	.429	14.5	Milwaukee	67	94	.416	36.5

ACKNOWLEDGMENTS

The author thanks the following baseball publicists for their prompt and efficient cooperation:

National League: Wayne Minshew, Atlanta; Bob Ibach, Chicago; Jim Ferguson, Cincinnati; Mike Ryan, Houston; Steve Brener, Los Angeles; Richard Griffin and Monique Giroux, Montreal; Jay Horwitz and Dennis D'Agostino, New York; Larry Shenk and Vince Nauss, Philadelphia; Ed Wade, Pittsburgh; Jim Toomey and Kip Ingle, St. Louis; Bill Beck, San Diego; Duffy Jennings, San Francisco.

American League: Bob Brown, Baltimore; Dick Bresciani, Boston; Tom Seeberg, California; Chuck Shriver, Chicago; Bob DiBiasio, Cleveland; Dan Ewald, Detroit; Dean Vogelaar, Kansas City; Tom Skibosh, Milwaukee; Tom Mee, Minnesota; Joe Safety, New York; Mickey Morabito, Oakland; Bob Porter, Seattle; John Blake and Dan Schimek, Texas; Howie Starkman, Toronto.

Other: Katy Feeney, National League; Phyllis Merhige and Bob Fishel, American League; and Rick Cerrone, Baseball Commissioner's Office.